TROUBLED SKIES

Crisis, Competition & Control in Canada's

Airline Industry

W9-CPY-514

Other Books by the Author

Global Pursuit: Canadian Business Strategies for Winning in the Borderless World

Hands Across the Ocean: Managing Joint Ventures (With a spotlight on China and Japan)

Trading: Inside the World's Leading Stock Exchanges

The Thomson Empire

Canadian Pacific: A Portrait of Power

Men of Property: The Canadian Developers Who Are Buying America

TROUBLED SKIES

Crisis, Competition &
Control in Canada's
Airline Industry

TROUBLED SKIES

First published in 1994 by
McGraw-Hill Ryerson Limited
300 Water Street
Whitby, Ontario, Canada
L1N 9B6

1 2 3 4 5 6 7 8 9 0 DWF 3 2 1 0 9 8 7 6 5 4

Canadian Cataloguing in Publication Data

Goldenberg, Susan, 1944–
    Troubled skies: crisis, competition and control
in Canada's airline industry

Includes index.
ISBN 0-07-551682-9

1. Air Canada. 2. PWA Corporation. 3. Airlines –
Canada – History. I. Title.

HE9815.A95G6 1994   387.7'06571   C 94-930546-4

Photographs reproduced by permission of *The Globe and Mail;*
Canadian Press; Canada's Aviation Hall of Fame (Reynolds – Alberta Museum)

Publisher: Donald S. Broad
Cover design: Mathews Communications – Design
Editorial services provided by Word Guild, Toronto

Printed and bound in Canada

To my parents

Contents

Acknowledgments

My deep thanks for the interviews given me by present and past management at the airlines, Cabinet Ministers, Members of Parliament and their executive assistants, union leaders, airline industry analysts, public interest groups, and lawyers. I very much appreciate their making time. My thanks also to Court officials for giving me access to cases.

S.G.

TROUBLED SKIES

Crisis, Competition & Control in Canada's Airline Industry

The Years of Vision (1919–1959)

Today's troubled skies are not what Canada's airline pioneers foresaw for the future. Their expectations were for a thriving industry. But seventy-five years after the beginnings of Canada's commercial aviation, the two major airlines – Air Canada and Canadian Airlines International, owned by PWA Corporation – are in grave distress.

From 1990 through 1992 they lost more money than they made in their entire histories. That is why each airline has attempted to save itself at the expense of the other in one of the longest and fiercest battles in Canadian corporate history. Both have also laid off thousands of workers.

But while the two major airlines' fight for survival is far from the glorious future the pioneers anticipated, they too had to grapple with many of the same issues.

The story begins in 1919 as ex-World War I pilots turned to peacetime flying, recording a number of firsts in Canada's aviation history. The first flight was made through the Rocky Mountains, from Vancouver to Calgary; as well, the first commercial flight – aerial surveying and fire patrol for Quebec timber companies – was made.

In addition, two Britishers – John William Alcock and Arthur Whitten Brown – made the first transatlantic flight from St. John's, Newfoundland to Clifden, Ireland, near Galway. According to the New York Times's account, they flew at 120 miles an hour, and the flight took 16 hours and 12 minutes. During much of the time, they were unable to see the sun, moon or stars due to the fog, and at one point, their plane almost spun into the water which, in a classic understatement, they described as an "unpleasant moment."

It was also in 1919 that the Canadian government began regulating aviation with the establishment of the federal Air Board to certify pilots and aircraft.

In that year, too, the Canadian Pacific Railway, formed in 1881 by an Act of Parliament, persuaded the government to extend its charter to permit it to operate an airline both within and beyond Canada's borders. It is worth noting that CPR's then president, Thomas Shaughnessy, was an American, as have been several key figures in Canada's airline industry.

Shaughnessy displayed enormous enterprise during his long career at the railroad. He joined it in 1882, one year after its incorporation, as the general purchasing agent. In 1884 and 1885, he helped save it from bankruptcy by placating its creditors. As president (1899-1918) and chairman (1918 until his death in 1923 at the age of seventy), he also greatly expanded the company's trackage, launched an Atlantic steamship service, and diversified into mining and smelting.

Yet, having obtained the right to establish an airline, the CPR did nothing about it for years. Into this vacuum stepped James Richardson, who would become known as "the father of Canadian aviation." Born in 1885, Richardson became president of his prominent family's Winnipeg grain firm in 1919. He also invested in mining ventures and it was his desire to develop northern Ontario's mineral wealth that prompted him to form Western Canada Airways (WCA) in 1926 with a personal stake of $200,000. He was convinced that airline transportation would enable the development of then-untapped mineral resources at least twenty years sooner than would otherwise have been possible because planes could fly in year-round. Hitherto, prospecting had been restricted to the summer months when the miners could reach otherwise inaccessible areas by canoe.

In 1927, under winter conditions and employing two open-cockpit aircraft without radio communication or weather navigational aids, WCA flew in fourteen men and thirty tons of supplies and equipment for the opening up of Churchill, Manitoba, during a thirty-day period. It was Canada's first major airlift and the federal government effusively described it as the most "brilliant operation in the history of commercial flying."

Over the next few years, WCA expanded beyond Northern Ontario west to the islands off the Pacific coast and north to the Arctic Ocean. Many of its flights were over uncharted territory, such as the entire two-thousand-mile length of the Mackenzie River stretching from northern Alberta through the Northwest Territories to the Beaufort Sea, a distance equivalent to that flown around the same time by Charles Lindbergh when he made the first solo transatlantic flight. Whereas Lindbergh received worldwide acclaim, scant attention was given to the Mackenzie River flight which proved to be of immense significance to the development of Canada's north. Previously, the Mackenzie River basin could be reached only by boat in summer and the occasional dog-sled trip in winter. Now, miners, fur traders and officials could travel in and out year-round. The planes also carried tons of supplies, including cattle and horses, canoes and heavy mining equipment.

Consequently, WCA rapidly became the world's leading air freight company, flying miners and supplies north, and furs and fish south. While WCA established the western portion of a potential trans-Canada airline, a number of aviation companies in Eastern Canada were experiencing financial and management problems. Their difficulties had aroused the interest of American companies, attracted by the possibility of gaining inexpensive entry to the Canadian market by buying these airlines at distress prices.

To ward off this threat, Richardson helped consolidate four of the struggling companies under the banner Aviation Corporation of Canada. A Canadian Pacific director, he convinced CP to become a shareholder, too. The logical next move was to merge WCA and Aviation Corporation, and this was done in 1930 under the name Canadian Airways. The new company had three shareholders – Richardson, CP and government-owned Canadian National Railways. Like CP, the CNR wanted to be a major player in more than one type of transportation.

At the start of the 1930s, Canada was one of the few countries that did not have a national airline. This was regarded as a serious deficiency by government and industry, especially as transportation had been recognized in Canada's earlier days – with the building of a national railway – as vital to the country's future. The government believed that by linking the vast distances between the Atlantic and Pacific oceans, transcontinental air transportation would increase the convenience of the travelling public and spur the development of a national economy. Such an east-west network would encourage self-reliance and lessen the influence of the United States.

Thus, in 1933 the Conservative prime minister, R.B. Bennett, asked Richardson if he would be interested in operating such an airline. Bennett wanted to prevent U.S. airlines, hungry for growth, from dominating Canada's skies, too. Although Canadian Airways' collection of regional operations was not interconnected, its coast-to-coast operations made it a logical candidate to operate a full trans-Canada airline.

Naturally, Richardson was interested. However, Bennett did not proceed because he believed it would be politically unwise to finance an airline during the Depression. "Desperate prairie farmers would hear the planes flying through skies blackened with the blowing dust of their drought-ruined farms," he explained.

The idea for a national airline, to be called Trans-Canada Air Lines (TCA), resurfaced with the election of the Liberals in 1935. Prime Minister Mackenzie King quickly established a Department of Transport to which he transferred control of civil aviation from the Department of Defence. As minister, he appointed a dynamo named Clarence Decatur Howe, another of the Americans influential in Canada's airline development. "He was an American who was a great Canadian," says retired Air Transport Association of Canada president Angus Morrison. "Howe liked to say, 'If I'm right 75 percent of the time, it's a pretty good average.'"

Born in Massachusetts, the brilliant Howe was just twenty-one when he was appointed an assistant professor of engineering at the Massachusetts Institute of Technology immediately after he graduated from there in 1907. The following year he accepted a post at Dalhousie University in Halifax as a full professor. In 1913, he became a Canadian citizen and was appointed chief engineer of the Board of Grain Commissioners of Canada, in charge of designing most of the federal government's largest grain elevators. It was quite an honour for a twenty-seven-year-old.

Three years later, in 1916, he formed his own company which designed grain terminals, wharves and factories in Canada, the U.S. and Argentina. The firm did extremely well; by the time Howe was elected to Parliament in 1935 at the age of forty-nine, he was one of the richest men in the House of Commons and the wealthiest in King's Cabinet. His business experience, intelligence, energy and toughness all helped him in the challenging task of developing a national airline.

At first it seemed the government intended Trans-Canada Air Lines to be jointly operated with private enterprise, since it proposed that ownership be evenly divided between the CPR, CNR and private aviation interests that each railway would nominate. In view of Canadian Airways being Canada's largest and most experienced airline with an established east-west transcontinental network, Richardson was confident it would be selected as the only private aviation interest and, subsequently, designated as Canada's national airline. He therefore began preparations, drawing up a detailed route system, buying planes, hiring more pilots, and sending crews for instrument flying training, still new in that era.

But Richardson was a victim of King's skill in equivocation. Although he appeared to advocate some private participation, King's real goal was government ownership, as became obvious from a clause Howe added six days later to the original proposal. The clause stated the government could buy out the company at any time. Also, it soon became apparent that Richardson's confidence was misplaced.

"Mr. Aviation" had made powerful enemies in the government. Since most people then had a fear of flying, the airlines' revenue primarily came from carrying post office mail. The post office claimed that Richardson quoted different rates to it and to Howe, and that his mail planes were too slow. Richardson maintained that the post office had confused his quotations with another bidder's. As for the planes, he said the post office was to blame because it had insisted he buy the very planes about which they complained.

Howe sided with the post office. The upshot was that the government-controlled CNR did not, as Richardson expected, nominate his firm as the private aviation representative. Instead, it backed a firm called British North American Airways, even though it was a shadow company with no planes. What it did have was leading Liberals as directors, including the postmaster-general's election campaign manager.

That government ownership, sometimes referred to as public ownership, was King's true aim became crystal clear when Howe stipulated that CP, the government, and government-owned CN each have equal board representation – a stipulation that he knew CP would find unacceptable. A war of words erupted between two forces accustomed to getting their own way – the government and Canada's most powerful corporation.

Canadian Pacific was then headed by Sir Edward Beatty. In 1918, six days before his forty-first birthday, he had become CP's first Canadian-born president; in 1924, he became chairman as well. He angrily objected that the government, which was not a direct investor, would have two-thirds control through both itself and CN, leaving CP, which would have invested half the money, with only one-third authority. Howe countered that since the government would be doing its share financially through providing airports and radio and meteorological services in addition to absorbing deficits, it was entitled to board membership despite no direct investment.

He had effectively manoeuvred Beatty into a position where Beatty had no choice but to reject participation. Beatty replied: "It is not, in the circumstances, necessary to continue our correspondence and I should appreciate it if, in the Bill as introduced, you would omit any reference to this company." But he graciously, if not sincerely, added: "I hope that your company will realize its highest hopes."

"Your" was the proper word, for Howe identified himself with Trans-Canada Air Lines, continuing to be responsible for it as he subsequently changed ministerial positions up until his 1957 retirement. He enjoyed being called "Mr. Airline." When an opposition M.P. once referred to TCA as a step towards socialism, Howe retorted: "That's not public enterprise; that's my enterprise." The TCA Act received Royal Assent on April 10, 1937 and Howe insisted on participating in TCA's July 30th, 17-hour, 11-minute (with four refueling stops) initial cross-country survey flight.

Did TCA become government-owned due to Howe's Machiavellianism, or because of Beatty's overweening pride? Probably both. The government's stipulation had its roots in King's deep distrust of the CPR because its majority ownership was then in the United Kingdom, and he suspected that its policy was really directed from London. Beatty's attitude was coloured by CP's resentment of the government's forming rival CN in 1923.

In later years when CP's own airline, Canadian Pacific Airlines, frequently lost money, CP executives sometimes wondered if Beatty should have accepted Howe's terms. Since he did not, the government offered a minority interest to both Canadian Airways and British North American Airways. They refused, too. Canadian Airways' James Richardson felt that Howe had betrayed his assurance that Canadian would be the cornerstone of a transcontinental service. In 1939, just two years after TCA was formed, Richardson died. "Nobody, including Howe, did as much for aviation in Canada as Richardson. Howe's government edicts upset what Richardson accomplished," says Donald Watson, who began his aviation career in 1938 at Canadian Airways and became president of Pacific Western Airlines in 1970.

Although criticized for making TCA a wholly-owned subsidiary of debt-ridden CN rather than a separate entity, Howe said it was logical because of parallel requirements for ticket offices, marketing and legal services. Initially, TCA agents were located at CNR ticket offices whose salespeople took over when they were off-duty.

Trans-Canada Air Lines began with working capital of $5 million. In an ironic twist, its first three planes, initial route and thirteen of its pilots were all obtained from Canadian Airways. For an airline intended to promote Canadianism, TCA began with decidedly American content. Its first route linked Vancouver and Seattle. It was not until the end of 1937 that flights between Canadian cities began with a Lethbridge-Winnipeg route. Also, most of TCA's senior management, including its chief operating officer, were American. Howe recruited them from U.S. airlines, primarily United.

Canadian Airways sold the three planes to TCA at cost – $169,176.70. Two were ten-passenger planes and the third was a small biplane (a plane with two-tiered wings). Air Canada (TCA's new name as of 1964) paid between $10 million and $60 million each for its current fleet of 115 jets, depending on type and size.

Not just plane prices have soared. TCA's first vice-president, operations, who ran the company, earned $17,500 (CN's president was also TCA's). Air Canada does not divulge salaries, but analysts estimate Hollis Harris, the current chairman, president and chief executive officer, receives around $500,000, about the same amount he made as chief executive officer at his former employer, Continental Airlines in the U.S. If so, it is considerably less than the approximately $600,000 earned per year by prominent lawyers. (And many lawyers have been employed by Air Canada and PWA in the current battles between them.) Harris's salary is also much lower than the $1 million – including bonuses and stock options – paid chief executives at the larger U.S. airlines.

TCA's first pilot made $400 a month; a senior Air Canada captain now receives $15,000 monthly. The Vancouver-Seattle fare was $14.20 round-trip when TCA took it over; today, full economy is $186 plus taxes; advanced discount booking rate, $104 plus taxes.

The first TCA flights were made under fairly primitive conditions. Its early planes had no oxygen, causing considerable discomfort for passengers and crews since the planes flew at 15,000 to 17,000 feet. Also, at first there were paved runways only at Montreal and Vancouver, and there was virtually no air traffic control.

Although finessed out of TCA, Canadian Pacific's Edward Beatty was determined that CP should be in the airline business. Timing was on its side. At the request of the British government, for eighteen months between 1940 and 1942 the company helped organize the North Atlantic Ferry Service whereby American and Canadian-built bomber planes were flown from Gander, Newfoundland to the United Kingdom. In addition, CP supplied railway cars as accommodation for the pilots who flew the planes across the Atlantic. The Ferry Service was taken over by the Royal Canadian Air Force in 1942.

In addition to its role in military aviation, by 1940 Canadian Pacific had purchased nine small regional airlines in western and northwestern Canada. These regional operations were known as "bush" companies because they flew through Canada's virtually unsettled northern forest land.

In 1941, CP, which was already a shareholder in Canadian Airways, became the full owner when it bought James Richardson's shares in that firm from his widow. All told, Canadian Pacific paid $4.2 million – less than TCA's start-up working capital of $5 million. In January 1942, Beatty consolidated the ten airlines under the name Canadian Pacific Airlines.

The "bush" companies are a colourful part of Canada's aviation history. The pilots were a diverse group of war veterans and teenagers obsessed with flying. Only people with a compulsion to fly could have endured the hardships. In the early days of open cockpit planes, helmets and goggles were the only protection for eyes and ears against bitterly cold temperatures (as much as eighty degrees Fahrenheit below zero). Canvas covers provided the only shelter when maintenance had to be done.

In winter, skis were attached to the planes for landing on thick snow and taking off through snowdrifts and from frozen lakes. There were no navigational aids, and maps were often incomplete with large sections marked "unexplored." Physical landmarks such as rivers, coastlines and railways pointed the way. As there was no network of airports for refueling, the pilots stocked gasoline cans at lakes chosen as bases.

Since there was no weather-forecasting service or radar, the pilots had to rely on the opinion of railway agents regarding the weather, with an agent at one station telegraphing the next for a description. A flag with a circle meant the weather was fine, a triangle indicated changeable conditions, and a cross warned of high risk.

The trips were often dangerous. John Jamieson, a bush pilot who later purchased Bradley Air Services, an Ottawa-based charter and cargo company, had the nerve-wracking experience of being stalked one hundred yards to his plane by a polar bear. "I walked in the hope the bear would; when I neared the plane I began to run and it did, too. I leaped in and started the engine, expecting the noise would halt the bear. But it continued to chase me as the plane took off."

Because they brought mail and supplies and were such an important link to the outside world, the bush pilots were greeted almost as heroes. One pilot had families in three far-apart communities! At these small lakeside outposts of tents and frame houses, the planes were tied to makeshift docks consisting of a thick piece of lumber. People from outlying areas paddled in by canoe and tied their canoes to the plane during the transfer of mail and cargo.

The pilots' departures were also major occasions. The men in the community put on their business suits, the women, their best dresses and fur wraps. The local Mountie, in dress uniform, was present. Children played on the shoreline as dozens of dogs raced among them. The pilot, dashingly clad in a windbreaker or leather jacket, jodhpur-style trousers and high leather boots, obligingly posed for pictures with the children, shook hands with the adults, loaded the cargo, donned his helmet and goggles, climbed into his plane, and took off for the next community.

The bush pilot companies bounced between profitability and bankruptcy. During World War II, business dried up as many northern mines closed. That is how Canadian Pacific was able to acquire nine bush companies so easily.

* * *

Shortly after forming Canadian Pacific Airlines, Beatty made a suggestion that would recur time and again right up to the present: merge with the other major airline. Theoretically, his proposal made sense since Canadian Pacific Airlines' north-south routes and TCA's transcontinental line would have fed traffic into one another. But his proposal was cold-shouldered because the government believed CP would benefit the most. Subsequently, Canadian Pacific Airlines tried to break into TCA's monopoly by applying for route licences that would have placed it in direct competition.

Canadian Pacific Airlines argued that it was "rendering far more vital air transportation than that provided by the publicly-owned airline which essentially parallels existing surface transport." Beatty died during the dispute, on March 23, 1943. Just a little over a week later, on April 2, King declared that TCA was the government's chosen instrument. "The government sees no good reason for changing its policy that TCA is the sole Canadian agency which may operate international air services," he said. "Within Canada, TCA will continue to operate all transcontinental systems and such other services of a main line character as may from time to time be designated by the government. Competition between air services over the same route will not be permitted, whether between publicly and privately-owned services or between two privately-owned services." Next, the government drafted legislation that would have required CP to divest its airline. The legislation was withdrawn when Canadian Pacific Airlines said it would stick to where it operated. The pressure tactics had succeeded.

The King decree became the basis of forty years of government regulation over starting an airline, routes, fares and service standards. It regarded its involvement as essential for an economic and efficient transportation system for all Canadians. As the 1989-1992 Royal Commission on National Passenger Transportation said, "By regulating the industry, by owning carriers, such as CN and its subsidiary, TCA, or by combining ownership and regulation, governments used transportation services to further public policy objectives. They believed that profits generated in passenger transportation markets should subsidize unprofitable ones."

In 1944, King initiated government regulation over routes with the establishment of the Air Transport Board to which air carriers would have to apply for route licences. The ATB's decisions were to be based on whether proposed routes would be in the public interest and whether operators had a reasonable chance of financial success.

The government's designation of TCA as the privileged airline put Canadian Pacific in the unaccustomed position of underdog, gaining it public sympathy in stark contrast to the antagonism its railway division had created by its perceived arrogance. Sympathizers overlooked that the CPR had begun life as the privileged railroad with land grants of 25 million acres, a $25-million cash subsidy (equivalent to close to $500 million in today's dollars) and the promise of a twenty-year monopoly on traffic in the area between the main line and the U.S. border.

Not only was Canadian Pacific Airlines drastically curtailed by King's edict, it also was nearly crippled by another government order stipulating that no new air routes other than those operated by the government would be awarded during World War II. The government explained that it wanted to prevent destructive competition so as to ensure there would be plenty of jobs in civil aviation for the returning air crews after the war. Maybe so, but the chief result of this prohibition was that TCA was able to grow at its rival's expense.

When the war ended, Canadian Pacific Airlines was a motley company ill-prepared to compete. It had eighty aircraft of twelve different types. Many were obsolete and lacked spare parts. (Ideally, airlines try to have as few types of planes as possible to avoid the expense of separate pilot training and of a vast assortment of parts.)

Canadian Pacific Airlines had the daunting task of melding ten companies into a harmonious whole – daunting because each company felt superior and had its own set of executives. "There was lots of blood on the hangar floor," recalls Ian Gray, an aeronautical engineer who joined the airline one year after its formation and became president from 1976 to late 1982. Some people were assimilated; others, unable to shake their previous independent style, left.

What the young airline needed for unity was a dynamic personality. Fortunately, there was such a person in its own ranks – Grant McConachie, one of the most remarkable figures in Canadian aviation. Born in 1909 in Hamilton, Ontario, McConachie grew up in Alberta. From his boyhood, he wanted to be a pilot and he worked as a locomotive fireman and at other jobs to finance flying lessons. He obtained a private pilot's licence in 1929 when he was twenty and a commercial pilot's licence a year later, and bought a used bush plane the next year with financial help from an uncle.

Like other bush pilots, he was pilot, engineer, mechanic, cargo loader and business negotiator. His first contract was to fly fish from northern Canada during the winter. The rest of the time he barnstormed prairie communities, doing stunt flying and giving short plane rides. In 1933, he formed United Air Transport, renamed Yukon Southern Air Transport in 1938. As chief pilot as well as president, he pioneered scheduled airmail and passenger service between Edmonton and Whitehorse in the Yukon, despite the inhospitable weather and terrain. Yukon Southern was also first in two important areas of airline safety: it was the initial western airline to use a radio compass in northern Canada and to fly multi-engined aircraft.

In 1940, Canadian Pacific purchased Yukon Southern as part of its ten-airline acquisition binge. McConachie steered clear of the clashes that broke out as the executives from the various airlines manoeuvred for power. In 1946, he was rewarded by being appointed assistant to the airline's president, W.M. Neal, who was also vice-president of Canadian Pacific. When Neal became president the following year, he promoted McConachie, then only thirty-seven, to president of the airline.

Handsome, engaging and far-seeing, McConachie had a phenomenal impact on Canadian Pacific Airlines. In 1942, its first year, its revenue had been $3 million; by 1964, twenty-two years later, and the year before McConachie's death, it had risen over twentyfold to $61 million. McConachie's vision was to transform the airline from a north-south operation across Canada into a transcontinental and international airline. If it took years for routes to become profitable, so be it, as long as the company achieved its goal. "I believe in making the bold move first; the profits will find their way home eventually," McConachie said. The airline's first international route, Vancouver to Sydney, Australia, was obtained in 1948 and took about twenty-five years to become profitable.

McConachie was liked and admired in the industry. "He was a capable, decent man who kept his word and had a tremendous sense of humour," says Angus Morrison, retired Air Transport Association of Canada president. "He was modest, too, making little of having rescued some people from an ice floe in the St. Lawrence River. As an ATAC member, he worked for the small as well as large carriers, saying, 'If we don't work on behalf of small carriers, we shouldn't take their fees.'"

Despite what Morrison says about his "decency," McConachie was no saint: he drank considerably (but was not a drunkard) and womanized, although married. But, in business, he became a legend, able to achieve the seemingly impossible through bravura and skill as a raconteur. "He operated on the principle that the gift of the gab baffles brains," Ian Gray recalls fondly. How many others would have had the audacity to wheedle Howe, Mr. TCA, into giving Canadian Pacific Airlines a Vancouver hangar at a bargain price as part of the disposal of government war assets after World War II, and then use that hangar to strengthen Canadian Pacific Airlines' position against TCA by centralizing maintenance and laying the foundation for international expansion? How did McConachie charm Howe? "Howe was an entrepreneur who liked entrepreneurs, and he admired McConachie's guts," Gray says.

McConachie was also skilled at handling Canadian Pacific executives, perturbed by the airline's teetering between borderline results and outright losses during McConachie's presidency. CP's chairman N.R. (Buck) Crump would laughingly remark that McConachie "promised the moon but never delivered." But, recalls Gray, McConachie was lucky, always able to bail himself out of awkward situations. "Once, when the boys in Montreal were breathing down McConachie's neck, he was able to lease one plane to Wardair for a year and another to somebody else," Gray says.

But charm and vision were not why the boys in Montreal indulged McConachie. Their indulgence was based on cold, hard facts. While spending heavily on planes for route expansion, McConachie was stringent about expenses. Dangling the lure of a brilliant future as compensation, he paid low salaries. Believing that free passes and good inflight service would generate word-of-mouth promotion, which he regarded as the best form of advertising, he spent little otherwise – for example, only $15,000 out of $9 million in revenue in 1950.

His financial controls made CP happy. So did the fact that for a company its size, the $4.2 million it paid for the ten companies that formed Canadian Pacific Airlines was infinitesimal. Moreover, since CP, rather than Canadian Pacific Airlines bought the airline's planes, it was CP that claimed the income tax capital cost allowance. Also, the airline obtained the bulk of its financing from its parent company and, when it came to paying interest, no sentiment was involved; CP charged prime-plus. And finally, when Pacific Western Airlines bought CP Air (as it had by then been renamed) in 1987, it paid CP $300 million.

The airline benefited CP non financially, too, because it gave the firm, which had a public relations problem with its railway, a good image. Thus, for thirty years the airline had a powerful ally in Ian Sinclair who enjoyed sharing a bottle of Scotch with McConachie and swapping stories. From his days as general solicitor with CP in 1953, then as president (1969-72) and chairman (1972-82), Sinclair provided continuity between CP and its airline. He championed the airline's public relations value. After CP pulled out of railway passenger transportation, he stressed that the airline "is something the public can put its finger on as being CP. It gives us great advertising value and pizzazz with the world."

Although Sinclair frequently complained that the airline "ran on gasoline and glamour" rather than profits, Ian Gray says that he enjoyed being part of the glamour. "When the railway side would say – correctly – that it could get a far greater return on investment on eight to ten locomotives than the airline from a DC-10 plane, Sinclair would support the argument of the airline's executives that to be competitive it must buy the plane," Gray says.

In 1948, while McConachie was settling in as Canadian Pacific Airlines' president, TCA also appointed a new president – Gordon McGregor. Born in 1901 in Montreal, he was eight years McConachie's senior. In comparison to McConachie's background and dazzling personality, McGregor's initially seems prosaic. But that was only half his personality; the other half thrived on adventure. On the prosaic side, McGregor graduated in engineering from McGill University in 1923 and then joined the Bell Telephone Company, working up from the engineering department to head office by 1938. The adventuresome side prompted him to begin flying in 1932, and by 1938 he was so skilled that he won an award as Canada's best amateur pilot. Then, as a group captain in the Battle of Britain, he was the oldest pilot to win the Distinguished Flying Cross.

After the war, McGregor joined TCA as general traffic manager. He made such a good impression that within three years he was promoted to president. Upon becoming president, he went to see Howe, who had wanted the TCA presidency. When Howe asked the reason for the appointment, McGregor said: "I expect I need some terms of reference." Howe replied: "You keep out of the taxpayer's pocket and I'll keep out of yours." During McGregor's twenty years as president, the airline's revenue soared from $32 million to $338 million and it suffered losses in only five years.

Whereas McConachie was extroverted, silver-tongued and a risk-taker, McGregor was reserved, plain spoken and cautious. As *The Ottawa Journal* once commented about the difference between them: "McGregor worries about balancing the books while McConachie concentrates on expansion and pizzazz." But, McGregor had a vision, too. Whereas McConachie advocated private enterprise, McGregor believed equally fervently that the public benefited from TCA's being a government monopoly.

As he wrote in his memoirs (published by Air Canada): "I think, basically speaking, that the whole idea of competition in industry is good. But to my mind there should be a clear-cut line between 'production' organizations and 'service' organizations dealing with public utilities, and the basic concept of monopoly should be accepted for the latter – consider municipal electricity and water supply, sewage and garbage disposal. . . . A monopoly is only a bad thing for the customer if it is abused. If the airline can be depended on to be forward-thinking, to be progressive, not to impose higher tariffs than necessary, then that is the cheapest way the service may be given. . . . It was a fallacy to suggest that TCA knew nothing about competition before CP Air was given transcontinental rights – we had been more than holding our own for years against the tough competition of U.S. services on trans-border routes, and numerous other trans-Atlantic carriers."

Unlike today's blood feud between the executives of Canada's two major airlines, McGregor and McConachie were friendly despite being archrivals. One story that illustrates this friendliness concerns McConachie's obtaining the Canada-Lisbon route after McGregor declined it. Subsequently, McGregor decided he wanted it. "Gordon, you're too late," said Howe. McConachie then tried to lessen McGregor's concern that the Lisbon route would divert some of TCA's London-bound traffic. To demonstrate the distance between the two routes, McConachie offered to inflate one of the stock of plastic globes he carried to promote his view that Canadian Pacific Airlines should be a global airline. "Don't bother," McGregor said smilingly, "That globe just blows up into whatever shape you want to demonstrate whatever point you're trying to make!"

When the presidencies of both began, TCA was already flying to London. Soon after, it was flying to the Caribbean, too. Gaining access was difficult because most airports there were under British control and the

British authorities wanted the business for government-owned British Overseas Airways Corporation (BOAC). They said "technical difficulties" made it necessary to keep out TCA. Canada's government monopoly was being blocked by the U.K. government's monopoly! But Howe's toughness broke the deadlock. As he was leaving a fruitless meeting in London with U.K. authorities, he remarked: "By the way, beginning Monday, the only Canadian airport which can be used by BOAC will be Quebec City." Quebec City's runways were too short for transatlantic aircraft, and as soon as Howe returned to his hotel, the British officials telephoned him that the Caribbean "technical difficulties" had been solved and TCA could immediately start flying there.

Although Canadian Pacific Airlines did not move its headquarters from Montreal, its parent's base, to Vancouver until 1949, its major hangar was there thanks to McConachie's arrangement with Howe. Thus, McConachie decided to focus on the Pacific as the first place to punch a hole in TCA's monopoly. International routes are negotiated bilaterally between countries, and McConachie applied to the federal government for routes Canada had obtained to Sydney, Australia, Hong Kong and Tokyo. "Do you really want them?" Howe asked. "Yes," replied McConachie. Then, since the government had decreed TCA was to be "the sole agency" in international flights, Howe asked McGregor if TCA wanted these routes. In one of those rash statements that come back to haunt people, McGregor replied: "Who would want to lose money on those routes? Let him lose it all and get out of our hair."

Believing that if Canadian Pacific Airlines did not fly to the Pacific the route would go by default to a foreign airline, Howe had the Air Transport Board grant it the routes, even though this contradicted the government's edict that TCA was to be "the sole agency" for international flights. Canadian Pacific Airlines began to fly to Sydney in 1948, and to Tokyo and Hong Kong in 1949.

TCA's management came to regard McGregor's rejection of the routes as the biggest mistake of his career and a severe restraint on TCA's global growth. It is the airline's self-exclusion from the Far East that was at the root of Air Canada's persistence throughout the years right up to the present that its international routes and those of its major competitor – first, Canadian Pacific Airlines, and then its buyer, PWA – be merged.

But at the time McGregor's decision made sense, especially as TCA had been unprofitable since 1946 and its immediate outlook was for further losses. It was unprofitable until 1950. There could well have been a public outcry about wasting taxpayers' money if McGregor had taken on the routes. Thirty years before it became mandatory, he was doing what the

1977 Air Canada Act demanded. The Act stipulated that the airline have "due regard to sound business principles and in particular the contemplation of profit." McGregor did not need this directive. "The public is apt to regard as a failure an organization that cannot make ends meet, and I think rightly so," he wrote in his memoirs. "A public service must not be a chronic money-loser." Still, his decision underscored the contrast between him and McConachie. To his critics, McGregor was overly cautious, whereas they considered McConachie visionary.

Canadian Pacific Airlines' Vancouver-Sydney route was a money-loser until the 1960s. But in the Far East, McConachie enjoyed his famed good luck. In 1949, the year McConachie obtained the Hong Kong route, the Communists took over mainland China, causing many Chinese to flee to Hong Kong and then onward to Canada via Canadian Pacific Airlines. Timing also favoured McConachie regarding Tokyo. He had negotiated the route with Douglas MacArthur, chief of the occupation forces in Japan after World War II and commander of the United Nations troops when the Korean War broke out in 1950. MacArthur, using every airline available, included Canadian Pacific Airlines in the flying of troops to the war zone. "Only McConachie could be that lucky," McGregor said wryly when the war began.

* * *

While McConachie and McGregor were expanding their airlines, the foundation for Pacific Western Airlines was being laid by Russell Baker, another former bush pilot with a vision of forming a major domestic and international airline. Born in Winnipeg in 1910, Baker's boyhood goal, like McConachie's, was to become a pilot. He was just sixteen when he began barnstorming in the prairies, and only eighteen when he flew the first airmail out of Winnipeg. He then moved to British Columbia where he flew more than seven hundred mercy missions as a bush pilot. Babies were born on his flights, murderers carried to justice, and injured people to hospitals, sometimes in howling blizzards.

During World War II, he did aerial survey work for the Alaska Highway that was jointly built by the U.S. and Canadian governments to provide access for U.S. soldiers in the event that the Japanese invaded Alaska, a concern of the Americans. When several U.S. bomber planes had to force-land in the mountains, Baker located them and, despite the difficult terrain and wintry weather, heroically flew out the survivors. For this rescue he was awarded the United States Air Medal.

In 1946, Baker co-founded Central British Columbia Airways (CBCA) with Walter Gilbert, a former Canadian Pacific Airlines superintendent.

Gilbert was president and Baker managing director. They were financed substantially by Karl Springer, a miner who had become dissatisfied with the inability of his own plane to carry large supplies to northern gold prospecting camps. Based at Fort St. James, 360 miles north of Vancouver, CBCA began with one plane and its first contract was to fly fire patrols for the British Columbia Forest Service.

Gilbert left CBCA in 1949 to start a B.C. fishing resort, so Baker became president, retaining the title of managing director. Subsequently, he acquired eight small B.C. and northwestern airlines. In 1953, to reflect the fact that he had assembled a group of western airlines that flew along the Pacific coastline, he renamed his company Pacific Western Airlines.

Handsome, as was McConachie, Baker shared McConachie's habits of heavy drinking and womanizing, although also married. The two sometimes went together on drinking and womanizing vacations. Their goal for their airlines was similar – to develop them into foremost transcontinental and international carriers. "I want PWA to become the first or second-largest airline in Canada, and for it to extend right across the world," Baker said. Whereas McConachie achieved his goal, Baker, who died when just forty-eight, did not. But PWA later fulfilled his ambition, thanks largely to its 1987 acquisition of CP Air.

But their similarities were only on the surface. McConachie lived comfortably; Baker, ostentatiously, in the largest house (a 28-room mansion) on the highest mountain overlooking Vancouver. He drove the biggest car and boasted of well-known people who had flown in his planes. Both he and his wife, Madge, liked to see their names in the newspaper society columns. What annoyed critics was his lavish spending at the very time he was borrowing heavily from the federal government's Industrial Development Bank to acquire competitors.

McConachie and Baker also differed in temperament. McConachie was popular due to his smooth-talking charm. In that era of government control over the awarding of routes, McConachie made a point of knowing bureaucrats by their first name. He also knew how to lose an argument graciously. He could laugh about the time he planned "to tell Howe a thing or two, but before I could, he told me a thing or two!"

By contrast, Baker was abrasive and hot-tempered. "He rode roughshod over people and had an inflated ego," says Angus Morrison. Even though PWA's future depended on good government relations to obtain routes, Baker engaged in tantrums that diminished PWA's chances. "He would pound his fist so hard on officials' desks that the glass top broke," says Donald Watson, who had the task of improving PWA's government relations after Baker's death. "Consequently, the bureaucrats would hide PWA's route application files behind their filing cabinets."

Baker's relations with Ottawa worsened after an incident involving an Air Transport Board inspector. When Baker was involved in a bitter take-over battle for Queen Charlotte Airlines, a West Coast rival, a Queen Charlotte executive complained to the Air Transport Board official of alleged irregularities in PWA's accounts. To check the complaint, the inspector seized some of PWA's books. Baker, who had many friends among the police, retaliated by having the police throw the inspector in jail. Naturally, this did not go over well in Ottawa. But Baker did succeed in acquiring Queen Charlotte Airlines in 1955 with the help of another Industrial Development Bank loan.

Both Canadian Pacific Airlines and PWA profited from the construction of the Alcan hydro-electric/aluminum smelter at Kitimat, British Columbia and from the Distant Early Warning (DEW) Line of radar stations built along the Arctic Coast of Alaska and Canada to detect aircraft from the then Soviet Union. Both projects required massive supply airlifts. Canada's Air Transport Board insisted that those from Canada be flown by Canadian carriers.

Simultaneous to expanding Canadian Pacific Airlines' domestic business, McConachie was adding international routes. When McGregor turned down the opportunity to extend Trans-Canada Air Lines' Toronto-Mexico City flight into South America, McConachie grabbed the rejected route just as he had when McGregor declined the Pacific routes. In return, he swapped some routes in Ontario and Quebec to TCA. Such swaps are common in the industry. Canadian Pacific Airlines began its first South America flight in 1955 from Vancouver to Lima, Peru via Mexico City.

But picking up TCA rejects was only one component of McConachie's international strategy. His vision called for circling the world from Sydney, Australia to Vancouver and onward via a Polar route to Amsterdam, a crossroads for travel in Europe. Going via the Pole would shorten the distance and flight time considerably, as compared to flying across Canada. With his trademark inflatable plastic globe and a piece of string, McConachie tirelessly demonstrated his plan and in 1955, the year Canadian Pacific Airlines started Vancouver-Lima flights, McConachie also obtained the Vancouver-Amsterdam route.

In 1957, Canadian Pacific Airlines began flights to Lisbon and Madrid. To fill return flights, McConachie devised an ingenious plan. He asked contractors at Alcan's Kitimat smelter and nearby Kemano port how many construction workers they needed. Then he advertised in newspapers in the Portuguese Azores Islands about the opportunities fishermen there would have at Kitimat-Kemano during their off-season. Many who came decided to settle in Canada. Subsequently, their families emigrated or they went home on visits, or both. It all generated business for Canadian Pacific Airlines.

Having diluted TCA's government-designated role as the "sole" international Canadian airline, McConachie renewed his efforts to shatter its domestic monopoly. His famed luck seemed to be on his side when the Conservatives, headed by John Diefenbaker, defeated the Liberals in 1957, and stayed in power until 1963. The Tories favoured private enterprise and competition and, as the Opposition, had criticized Air Canada's monopoly. George Hees, whom Diefenbaker appointed transport minister, believed TCA was a "spoiled child."

Thus McConachie, confident the Conservatives would allow Canadian Pacific Airlines to compete transcontinentally, filed an application to the federal Air Transport Board in 1958 for three cross-country routes and two partial ones. The three national routes were Vancouver-Calgary-Saskatoon-Ottawa-Montreal; Vancouver-Edmonton-Montreal; and Vancouver-Winnipeg-Toronto-Montreal. The partial ones were Edmonton-Regina-Toronto and Winnipeg-Ottawa-Montreal.

So confident was McConachie that he underestimated warning signs that the market would not be opened to the extent he wished. These warning signs appeared in a report commissioned by Hees from a British transportation expert, Stephen Wheatcroft. Wheatcroft concluded that only three routes could withstand competition without Trans-Canada Air Lines and Canadian Pacific Airlines suffering financially. The three were Toronto-Montreal, Vancouver-Victoria, and Toronto-Winnipeg – a recommendation that bore little similarity to McConachie's proposal.

McConachie was not alone in applying for transcontinental routes. PWA's Baker did so, too. Then, a week before the ATB was to begin hearings on both applications, Baker withdrew PWA's. It was not because PWA would necessarily have lost. What was apparent was that only one or the other would win because Wheatcroft's report said that "the provision of a scheduled transport service is inevitably duplication or oligopolistic. The conditions of supply cannot, except in rare cases, allow more than a very small number of carriers to serve any specific route." PWA might have won since Baker proposed all-jet service and McConachie only piston engines. McConachie was soured on jets because one he had ordered in 1949 had crashed, as had another in 1953. Canadian Pacific Air Lines did not begin jet service until 1959.

McConachie and Baker loved deal-making, and they drew up a pact that each thought would benefit his airline. In return for Baker's withdrawing PWA's application and supporting that of Canadian Pacific Airlines, McConachie agreed to turn over the lucrative Mackenzie River route that he had built up through northern Alberta to the Northwest Territories to PWA – if his airline obtained a transcontinental route.

McConachie was so certain he would succeed in the Tory free-enterprise climate that he did insufficient homework for the ATB hearings. He should have expected Air Canada to object strenuously to his application because its transcontinental monopoly was its chief moneymaker. Profits on its transcontinental route, and to a lesser extent on its overseas routes, made up for losses in all others. Although King had intended TCA to be a mainline operation and private enterprise to fly local routes, TCA acquired an increasing number of local runs to smaller communities, particularly in the Liberal regions of Atlantic Canada, Quebec and Northern Ontario. These routes were money-losers, although they did feed traffic into the transcontinental run.

However, TCA tried to portray itself as a protector of the public interest, rather than as a money-hungry business. It argued that lack of competition actually benefited consumers. "Duplication of efforts and facilities from competitive service tend to increase the end cost of the product and therefore increase the cost to the consumer," Gordon McGregor said. "Who would think of having a municipality with two sources of lighting supply, two sources of sewage disposal, or two sources of garbage collection? It doesn't make good economic sense."

McConachie's mistake in being so nonchalant had its parallel in McGregor's error a decade earlier about the Pacific routes. When Air Canada resisted his application with reams of opposing data, McConachie was caught unprepared. Reflecting his optimistic nature, he had brought along overly bullish traffic forecasts which depended, as Ian Gray says, "on keeping all our planes in the air at one time." After four days of Air Canada's demolishing McConachie's material, CP chairman Buck Crump had Ian Sinclair, then CP's general solicitor, take over the questioning of TCA's witnesses. Both TCA and CP officials agreed that Sinclair's intervention prevented Canadian Pacific Airlines from losing. He was rewarded in 1960 by being named vice-president and general counsel, placing him on the path to CP's presidency.

Sinclair's challenge was to show that a rival transcontinental service would not cost Canadian taxpayers dearly in the form of TCA deficits. He argued this would not happen if TCA increased its efficiency, but the ATB disagreed that TCA was inefficiently run.

The hearings were in their second month when the industry was stunned by the death of Russell Baker on November 15 from a third heart attack; he was just forty-eight. Although not a Roman Catholic, Baker had many Catholic clergy as friends. A requiem mass was sung for him in Vancouver's

Holy Rosary Cathedral on November 17. Then, two PWA planes flew his body and a contingent of family, friends and company officials to Fort St. James for his funeral service and interment. Baker had maintained homes in both Vancouver and Fort St. James where he had started Central British Columbia Airways.

The following month, on December 31, the ATB granted Canadian Pacific Airlines only one route – Vancouver-Winnipeg-Toronto-Montreal – and only one flight a day. Although a very modest victory, it did crack TCA's monopoly.

For Canadian Pacific Airlines the question was whether it had won too little to make going transcontinental worthwhile. The return on investment would be poor because three planes were needed – one for each direction plus a spare. However, not to proceed would have preserved TCA's domestic monopoly. Therefore, McConachie went ahead, beginning transcontinental service in May 1959. To attract customers, he offered lower fares on a greater percentage of seats than TCA previously had. Of course, McConachie only had to offer his discounts on one return flight.

McConachie honoured his pledge to Baker to hand over the Mackenzie River routes to PWA. It turned out to be one of Baker's best deals, as these routes more than doubled PWA's revenue-producing miles.

By 1960, the vision of McGregor, McConachie and Baker had made air travel a way of life for all Canadians, rather than for only the few as in the industry's pioneering years. In 1938, the year after TCA was formed, 105,000 Canadians travelled by plane; in 1960, five million. Air freight volume also grew enormously – from eight million kilograms in 1938 to 135 million kilograms in 1960. After 1960, however, turmoil began to beset the industry.

CHAPTER TWO

The Years of Turmoil (1960 –1979)

In 1960, just one year after Canadian Pacific Airlines began to compete on cross-country flights, the president of rival Trans-Canada Air Lines, Gordon McGregor, proposed that the two airlines merge. His proposal was a forerunner of the several merger overtures between 1991 and 1993 by Air Canada (TCA's name since 1964) to its chief competitor, PWA, which had purchased CP Air in 1987.

Not only would the merger McGregor suggested have made domestic air travel a monopoly once again, it also would have absorbed Canadian Pacific Airlines' lucrative international routes. While TCA carried double the number of people internationally, the average overseas passenger on Canadian Pacific Airlines travelled almost twice as far. Thus, its international revenue almost equalled TCA'S.

Like today's Air Canada executives, McGregor portrayed a merger as being in Canada's best interest. "The advantages to the country and the industry in airline service and economics were potentially immense," he wrote in his memoirs. "With only one main line and international carrier, bilateral agreements could have been negotiated from strength and wasteful competition in international routes eliminated, enabling Canada to compete more vigorously with foreign flag carriers. Planned expansion programs would have been based on economic and national considerations only. Scheduling and connections could have been improved, and consolidation of personnel, equipment, facilities and services would have produced substantial economies and simplified operating problems."

Donald Gordon, chairman of Canadian National, TCA's parent, went further, maintaining that if Canadian Pacific, Canadian Pacific Airlines' owner, rebuffed the merger proposal, the government should insist on the absorption of Canadian Pacific Airlines by TCA. CP did refuse, and the Diefenbaker government did not do what Gordon wanted.

While Canadian Pacific Airlines fended off Trans-Canada Air Lines, Pacific Western Airlines was in turmoil following Russell Baker's death. It was both short of cash and embroiled in personality conflicts. To strengthen its balance sheet, PWA sold some planes. It halved the number of types in its fleet to achieve cost savings through bulk buying of parts and reduced pilot training time. (Pilots have to be trained on each type of plane in an airline's fleet.)

PWA board of directors' meetings often degenerated into anarchy. Baker's widow, Madge, would toss cups of coffee at directors with whom she disagreed. Perhaps she was emulating her husband who, when drunk, had thrown furniture out of windows. Karl Springer, who had backed the formation of Central British Columbia Airways, PWA's forerunner, took over the presidency after Baker's sudden death. But as his chief interest was mining, he was largely a figurehead.

A power struggle erupted between Baker's two heirs apparent: Duncan McLaren, executive vice-president in charge of scheduled operations, and Dick Laidman, vice-president and general manager, in charge of bush operations. Laidman was supported by Madge Baker. In February 1961, the struggle culminated in McLaren's ouster.

Within months PWA was facing a new crisis. Its future as an independent airline was threatened when Karl Springer secretly attempted to unload his stock through a merger with Transair, a Winnipeg-based regional airline to which PWA had lost its Distant Early Warning Line business. Without notifying the board of directors or management of his intention, Springer made an appointment for this purpose in November 1961 with Transair's owners.

PWA's management learned of his plans from Rusty Harris, the vice-president of finance whom Springer had telephoned at 3:30 a.m., telling him to meet him at Vancouver's airport at 6:00 a.m. "Where are we going? Do I need a toothbrush, a change of shirt, any papers?" Harris asked. "Just come," Springer replied. They flew to Winnipeg and went to Transair's headquarters. When Springer reached a handshake deal to sell his shares to Transair, Harris rushed to a pay telephone to alert Laidman and Donald Watson, a vice-president whom Baker had hired shortly before his death. "Get going, or Springer will sell us out," Harris urged.

Since the money to buy out Springer had to be raised instantly, both Laidman and Watson strove to find a rescuer in the hope that at least one of them would succeed. Watson tried to contact Montagu Black, known to today's generation as the father of media magnate Conrad Black. Black was one of Canada's wealthiest men with extensive private investments. Watson failed to reach him through a mutual acquaintance, a hotelier who was a hunting and fishing friend of Black.

But Laidman's search was successful. He convinced Bruce Samis, a Vancouver investment dealer, to buy out Springer. Born in 1909 and a contemporary of Baker, Samis was the son of a prominent banker. He had started his own investment firm in 1940. He paid Springer $260,000. Thirteen years later, when the Alberta government bought PWA, these shares were worth $9.3 million!

Samis brought stability to PWA. He became chairman, made Laidman president, and replaced the entire board, including Madge Baker, with experienced businesspeople. The management crisis was over, but financial problems loomed. Just before PWA had to meet its December 15 payroll, the Royal Bank of Canada, concerned about an expired PWA commitment, withdrew as PWA's principal banker. The new board and management had to come up with the payroll money themselves. Some board members were clients of the Canadian Imperial Bank of Commerce; through their contacts the CIBC became PWA's new chief banker. Additionally, Samis obtained a substantial loan from the federal Industrial Development Bank to pay off short-term indebtedness.

* * *

While PWA was straightening itself out, Canadian Pacific Airlines' president Grant McConachie was planning how to further break Air Canada's monopoly. After the Liberals under Lester Pearson returned to power in 1963, McConachie pleaded with J.W. (Jack) Pickersgill, the minister of transport, to make his airline an official flag carrier like Air Canada. Interestingly, Pickersgill's executive assistant was R.A. (Sandy) Morrison who is now Air Canada's vice-president, corporate communications, government and industry relations.

In 1964, Pickersgill did as McConachie had asked, assigning each airline separate portions of the world. To Canadian Pacific Airlines he gave the South Pacific, South America and southeast Europe, plus the north European gateway of Amsterdam. To Air Canada he allotted the rest of Europe, the British Isles and the Caribbean. Since these routes were identical to each airline's existing ones, Pickersgill's designations merely ratified the status quo. Africa, in which neither was interested, and the United States, with which bilateral negotiations were still pending, were excluded.

McConachie had little time to enjoy this triumph; in June 1965, he died of a heart attack at age fifty-six. "He was a perfect example of burning the candle at both ends – he played hard and worked hard," Ian Gray says.

McConachie had not groomed a successor, and the company was unprepared because the severity of McConachie's heart condition had not been known. The person appointed to succeed him, Jack Gilmore, was his complete opposite. Unlike McConachie, who was a pilot and enjoyed visiting the airline's hangars at midnight to check mechanics' work, Gilmore was an accountant chosen to improve the company's borderline finances. After four years at Canadian Pacific, Gilmore had joined Canadian Pacific Airlines in 1949, in its seventh year, as assistant comptroller. He became comptroller in 1956. He was also a founding member of the Fraser Institute, a Vancouver economic and social research centre. On succeeding the legendary McConachie, he realistically remarked: "When you're right, you're bright. If you're wrong, you're ruined."

Gilmore was not ruined – nor did he try to be another McConachie. Unlike McConachie, he preferred numbers to fraternizing with federal government bureaucrats. Whereas McConachie flew to Ottawa weekly, Gilmore went "only if pushed," Gray says. By contrast, since Air Canada's headquarters are in Montreal, its executives have far less distance to travel to Ottawa. Gray believes Gilmore's lack of rapport with Ottawa officials put Canadian Pacific Airlines "behind in the political game" to obtain more transcontinental business because the bureaucrats largely determined route designations.

Notwithstanding Gray's comments, Gilmore did meet with some success. When the Canada-U.S. negotiations were completed in 1966, Canadian Pacific Airlines obtained the Vancouver-San Francisco route. However, the more profitable Montreal-Toronto-Los Angeles route went to Air Canada. Also, Air Canada began to advertise joint fares with U.S. carriers to Honolulu, a point served directly by Canadian Pacific Airlines. But the following year brought gains for Canadian Pacific Airlines when Pickersgill widened domestic competition by allowing the airline up to a 25 percent share of transcontinental traffic.

Pickersgill had a major impact on the airline industry in other ways as well. In 1967, the same year he increased transcontinental competition, he was responsible for the passage of The National Transportation Act. The first federal law to encompass all modes of transportation, it emphasized the need for competition between air, rail, truck and bus carriers to achieve an "economic, efficient and adequate transport system." However, regulatory restrictions on routes and fares were retained.

As its enforcement arm, the Act created the Canadian Transport Commission (CTC) which consolidated the previous separate boards for the individual transportation sectors, including the Air Transport Board. Its functions were transferred to the CTC's Air Transport Commission. Pickersgill was appointed as the first president. Under the 1987 National Transportation Act, the CTC was replaced by the National Transportation Agency. In May 1993, the Agency approved AMR's proposal to invest in Canadian Airlines International.

As the 1960s drew to a close, it was Air Canada's turn to plunge into turmoil. Its civil war began after Gordon McGregor retired as president in

May 1968 after holding this position for twenty years; during this time Air Canada had doubled in size every five years. Pierre Trudeau had just succeeded Pearson as prime minister and, since Air Canada was a Crown corporation, it was up to the government to appoint a successor. Trudeau's choice sparked years of trouble. He decided to appoint a French Canadian – Yves Pratte – as chairman to placate growing nationalist sentiment in Quebec. Trudeau had never met Pratte who was well regarded in Quebec. A lawyer practising in Quebec City, Pratte had previously been dean of Laval University's faculty of law and special legal adviser to the Quebec government under both the provincial Liberals and the Union Nationale. Thus, Pratte had an impressive background. The drawback was that he had no experience in the airline industry.

As president in charge of daily operations, Trudeau appointed John Baldwin who had been deputy minister of transport for many years. Baldwin had played an influential role in the limited transcontinental share obtained by Canadian Pacific Airlines in 1958 through urging then Transport Minister George Hees to study the economic ramifications if it were to obtain more. Air Canada employees were disgruntled at qualified people within the company being overlooked in favour of what they regarded as purely political appointments.

The situation Pratte walked into bears a striking resemblance to Air Canada's recent problems, notably the overstaffing that a Crown corporation mentality creates. Responsibilities were ill-defined and redundant. Also, interdepartmental rivalries were rampant. There was insufficient planning and too little emphasis on profit. When Pratte hired the McKinsey Company, the world-famous U.S. management consulting firm, to recommend how Air Canada's management could be restructured, head office employees were cast into uncertainty about their future.

Having alienated a great many people in management, Pratte soon came into conflict with Air Canada's machinists. They wanted a 20 percent wage increase for parity with their U.S. counterparts. Considering that the Trudeau government had established voluntary wage-hike guidelines of 6 percent to 7 percent annually, it was impossible for Air Canada, as a Crown-owned corporation, to pay the machinists what they wanted. However, Pratte did offer 8 percent for the first year, slightly more than the government's suggested ceiling. But for the second year he offered only 6 percent, so that the average of the two years would meet the government's guideline. Not satisfied, the machinists went on strike on April 20, 1969. After thirty days they settled for 8 percent each year. The strike cost Air Canada $40 million in lost revenue and helped CP Air and the regional airlines to gain customers.

After the machinists returned to work, employees' anxiety continued to grow as to what the McKinsey report would recommend. Their worst fears were realized on January 30, 1970 when Pratte announced a sweeping reorganization. Its main thrust was to end the division between the separate fiefdoms of operations and sales so that their work would be coordinated. Vice-presidencies of marketing, customer service, strategic planning, computer and systems services, schedule planning, and personnel and industrial relations were created to make certain the coordination occurred.

The restructuring brought Air Canada into the modern age of business management. But because the reorganization was imposed unfeelingly, shocked employees referred to the day of Pratte's announcement as Black Friday. Most executives were excluded from consideration for the new positions; instead, mainly outsiders were appointed. Division heads selected people for their departments from names on magnetic tags on charts posted at Air Canada's headquarters – a humiliating process. About 350 managers found themselves displaced. Survivors had to learn their new jobs on their own since the previous incumbents had left the company or were reassigned.

* * *

While Air Canada was enmeshed in the turmoil generated by its massive reorganization, Pacific Western Airlines was also undergoing dramatic change. In October 1970, PWA's board forced Dick Laidman, president since 1961, to resign because PWA was headed for its first loss since 1962.

Donald Watson, who had been with PWA since 1958, was appointed as the new president. He had an impressive background. Born in 1921, Watson was only a boy when he decided his goal was to became a pilot. By the age of fourteen he was a flying apprentice, and by the time he was nineteen he had soloed a plane and earned an air engineer's licence. Between 1938 and 1940 he was an engineer at James Richardson's Canadian Airways. During World War II, the Canadian government hired him to work on the British Commonwealth Air Training Plan which trained wartime aircrews. In 1945, the United States Air Force hired him to do similar work.

After World War II, Watson helped found the Saskatchewan government's Air Ambulance Service. During his three years there, the Service transported more than six thousand patients, often in harsh weather, from far-flung outposts in nearly inaccessible locations to major medical centres. Then, in 1949, Watson joined Ontario Central Airways, a Northern Ontario airline, where he became managing director and a partner.

Watson's joining PWA was the result of a chance encounter with Russell Baker in October 1958, one month before Baker's death. Watson had been in British Columbia studying a local airline's performance on behalf of the federal Industrial Development Bank.

"As I was passing PWA's airport office in Vancouver, Baker called out of his window to come and see him," Watson recalls. "He then asked me to join PWA. I said 'No', explaining that 'different engines drive us. For example, your practice of coming in at noon and going home at 2:00 a.m. doesn't fit my desire to have a home life with my family.'"

After assuring Watson he could have regular hours, Baker asked what salary he wanted. "When I told him, he said only one person made that much at PWA – himself," Watson continues. "He offered slightly less. Then, there was the matter of title. Baker's habit was to pay low salaries and hand out titles as compensation. We settled on 'assistant to the president,' with the promise that I would become general manager in six months. Baker called in Duncan McLaren, then his executive assistant, to draw up a memo with a copy for each of us."

Prior to starting his new job on November 17, 1958, Watson was staying with his family at a Vancouver motel. He was stunned when he looked at the front page of the Saturday, November 15 morning newspaper. "The left column had a big story about Baker's sudden death at 3:00 a.m.," Watson recollects. On reporting in at PWA on Monday, he had an unpleasant surprise. Karl Springer, who had taken over as president, did not know Baker had hired Watson and refused to accept him until Duncan McLaren showed him Baker's memo. While McLaren and Dick Laidman fought for the presidency, Watson kept his "head down in the trenches," holding most of PWA's vice-presidential positions including operations, technical services and government relations.

During Watson's six-year presidency, PWA's profit surpassed $1 million for the second time in its history and then $2 million for the first time. Watson achieved these results through expansion rather than retrenchment. To achieve this expansion he decided PWA needed to modernize its fleet and he turned for assistance to Duncan McLaren who was well-placed to help since he was then in California selling planes. He introduced Watson to U.S. banks and corporate sources of funds such as General Electric and Pepsi-Cola credit corporations.

To obtain their backing, Watson had to present a good case concerning PWA's earnings potential. He argued that it would be improved by PWA's "moving round the world" with charter passenger plus cargo flights. "PWA should not stay hunkered down in Canada because its opportunities are limited due to government regulation preventing it from operating transcontinentally," he said.

PWA soon began offering inclusive tour charters in which hotel rooms, meals and sightseeing were totally or partially included in the fare. Watson was equally energetic in developing new cargo business. He bought five planes to carry freight and "went out and developed the markets." PWA became involved in such novel projects as relief supply airlifts for distant places like Bangladesh and Katmandu in Nepal. He also established cargo runs in Southeast Asia and from Frankfurt to Lebanon, Kuwait, Iran, India and Tokyo. One year after Watson became president, PWA was doing business in fifty-two countries and had a $1.4-million profit compared to a $163,000 loss in 1970. The company's revenue doubled between 1970 and 1974.

PWA's progress did not go unnoticed. In June 1974, Federal Industries, a diversified Winnipeg firm, informed Watson it wanted to buy 60 percent of PWA through White Pass and Yukon Railway of which Federal had acquired control the previous year. Federal delegated White Pass as the buyer because both it and PWA were Vancouver-based. When Watson adamantly said PWA was "not for sale," the Federal Industries representative replied: "It would have been nice to do it on a friendly basis, but we can still buy." To which Watson retorted: "It'll be more difficult than you think." He proceeded to remind Federal that since it already was in the transportation business, it had to obtain approval from the Canadian Transport Commission. The tactic worked – Federal rejected the opportunity to gain tactical control of PWA through purchasing a block of PWA shares larger than those held by major PWA shareholders while waiting for the CTC to decide.

During this time, a surprise contender was secretly planning a counter-bid – the Alberta government. Peter Lougheed, Alberta's Progressive Conservative premier since 1971, considered acquiring PWA as extremely important to his overall strategy "to diversify Alberta's economy so that it would be less dependent on oil and gas, although it would still be a primary industry." He believed ownership of PWA would help fulfill his mission to make Alberta the "gateway to the North," increase the export of Alberta's agricultural products through air-freight service around the world, and make the province a more attractive place in which to establish head or representative offices, hold conventions and vacation.

In particular, Lougheed was concerned that if British Columbia-based White Pass took over PWA, it would develop a north-south traffic corridor through British Columbia, thereby undermining Alberta's aim to be the foremost "gateway to the North." His apprehension intensified when Stuart Hodgson, commissioner of the Northwest Territories, "told me, unprompted, at a luncheon where we happened to meet, 'You have to acquire PWA or Alberta will lose its position as the gateway to the North.'"

Lougheed, however, did not immediately react by deciding that the Alberta government should buy PWA. He hesitated because he knew he "would have difficulty with some in our Party because the Progressive Conservatives are a free-enterprise Party." Thus he suggested to Fred Peacock, minister of industry and commerce, that he attempt to interest Alberta businesspeople in making a better offer than that of White Pass and Yukon Railway. Among those Peacock canvassed was Ron Southern, a prominent Calgarian who was a director of PWA and whose firm, Calgary-based ATCO Industries, was a substantial PWA shareholder. Southern declined on the basis that the type of offer he thought most equitable – one which would include all shareholders, not just controlling ones – would be too costly. Other businesspeople were not interested because of the magnitude of the financing that would be involved, especially as financing costs were then high.

In view of the situation, Peacock told Lougheed that a purchase by the Alberta government was the only available alternative. Thereupon on July 22, Lougheed called a tactical meeting of his senior Cabinet officials, including Peacock and Don Getty, the minister of intergovernmental affairs and chairman of the Cabinet's economic planning and transportation committee. Because of the warm weather that day, the meeting was held on the patio of Lougheed's office causing the participants to code-name their takeover "Operation Patio."

In order to outmanoeuvre White Pass, Lougheed requested that the takeover plan be developed quickly – and it was. It was ready eight days later, on July 30. Lougheed then had to convince his party that the takeover was a good idea. It was a difficult task. "It was an extreme move for a free-enterprise party and the right wing – which was large in numbers – resisted," he recalls. "I argued that Alberta, as a landlocked province, had to take bold action to control its destiny." Not everyone, however, was persuaded by this sales pitch. Therefore, Lougheed promised that the province would not own PWA in perpetuity but would eventually privatize it, although he refrained from saying when. "Did I have to make a deal with the right wing that I would eventually sell PWA in return for their supporting the purchase? I'd put it that by saying my intention was to privatize PWA minimized resistance from the right wing," he laughingly recollects.

Just one day after Lougheed convinced the Conservatives to support the purchase, his government went into action. Early in the morning of Wednesday, July 31 Getty instructed R.B. Love, a Calgary lawyer retained by the government to negotiate the purchase, to proceed. Love then called Ron Southern, saying he was acting for an undisclosed client interested in buying PWA. He asked Southern to telephone PWA chairman Bruce Samis to accept a call from Love in which Love would request an urgent meeting of PWA's directors. Samis agreed to assemble the directors for a meeting at 2:45 p.m. Vancouver time in his office in the Toronto-Dominion tower.

At the meeting Love still would not divulge his client's name but went so far as to say that it was a substantial client prepared to buy all of the shares and not just 51 percent, "which would have left the rest out to dry," as Watson puts it. Love also said his client would pay well – almost five dollars more a share than the prevailing price.

"At that price, we couldn't stop the takeover; all we could ask was whether the acquisitor would retain management and the airline's objectives and he said it would," Watson recalls. "By then, it was 2:00 a.m. The lawyer called his client and then said he was authorized to disclose that it was the Alberta government." The takeover offer was revealed two days later. "That's how things happen at the O.K. Corral," Watson says, in a wry reference to the famous gunfight.

But just a week later the takeover was in jeopardy when the federal government challenged Alberta's right to make the purchase without Ottawa's approval. it maintained that federal air carrier regulations required Alberta to obtain approval from the Canadian Transport Commission. Alberta contended the regulations applied only to a "person" and not to it because a province was not a person. The case was first heard by the Federal Court of Appeal which supported the federal government's interpretation. But it was overruled by the Supreme Court which accepted Alberta's definition.

Considering that the federal government owned Air Canada, its effort to prevent Alberta from also owning an airline may seen illogical. However, what was at stake was not government ownership but jurisdictional and regulatory control. The dispute arose when the Alberta and Trudeau governments were battling over the direction and control of Canada's energy policy, and the federal government regarded the PWA purchase as yet another instance of Alberta's trying to undermine its authority.

As PWA was being transformed into a Crown corporation, the turmoil precipitated by the Pratte reorganization escalated at Air Canada. Believing they had been treated shamefully, many employees lost their sense of esprit de corps. Unfortunately for consumers, some of this frustration was vented on them through rudeness, mislaid baggage and a large increase in late flights. Naturally, Canadians began to grumble about their taxes going to support a company that treated them so cavalierly. These innocent victims of Air Canada's malaise were incensed that there were limited alternatives due to government regulations assigning Air Canada the bulk of transcontinental traffic.

Having angered employees and the public, Air Canada infuriated yet another important constituency – travel agents – by becoming a shareholder in a Montreal travel agency. The marketing vice-president who conceived this idea wanted to lessen the airline's dependence on outside agreements. The agents, however, maintained Air Canada had invaded their turf. Backpedalling rapidly, Air Canada officials said the vice-president had acted on his own, without executive committee approval.

Public grumbling intensified when it became known that the same vice-president was not making mortgage payments on a villa he had bought at a Barbados resort; the airline had been using the villa on its charter tour operations. He denied doing anything wrong, explaining that he had not wanted to begin payments until he received title to the house and that he would be paying full price. But his protestations were in vain; he was forced to resign.

When faced with actual or apparent scandals, governments try to deflect public fury by appointing Royal Commissions, and this was what the Trudeau government did. The Commission cleared Air Canada's financial conduct but Otto Lang, then minister of transport, demanded Pratte's resignation. In his resignation letter of November 28, 1975, Pratte wished his successor well, writing: "I know that he will have the support of the employees of Air Canada; I only hope he will have that of the Government."

In that Pratte was a Quebecker, Trudeau decided his successor should be, too, so as not to alienate French Canadians at a difficult time in Federal-Quebec relations following the FLQ crisis of 1970. He therefore appointed Canadian National's chairman, Pierre Tachereau, a reversion to the practice of the chairman of CN, Air Canada's parent, holding the same position at the airline.

John Baldwin, who had been appointed president when Pratte was made chairman, had retired in 1974. The government had learned its lesson that Air Canada's employees resented the filling of top jobs with outsiders. Thus, it chose as his successor a popular, longtime employee named Claude Taylor who had worked his way up through the ranks. Born in 1925 into a New Brunswick farming family, Taylor joined the airline in 1949 when it was just twelve years old. He began as a passenger ticket agent in Moncton. A year later, he was transferred to Montreal as a clerk. After work he attended McGill University's extension department and graduated as an accountant in 1953.

Taylor says he joined Air Canada because "it was a brand new industry and I was fascinated by it." He was later offered a position by a U.S. airline, the name of which he will not disclose, although he does say it was not American Airlines, the airline with which Air Canada battled from 1991 to 1994 for a link with Canadian Airlines International. Taylor preferred to remain in Canada. "I'm a Maritimer and Canadian and wanted to work for Canadian industry," he says.

Through promotion after promotion, Taylor became general manager of marketing services in 1964 and went on to become the first person to hold the position of vice-president, strategic planning, created by the Pratte-commissioned McKinsey report. Later, he became vice-president, government and industry affairs and subsequently vice-president, public affairs. As president from 1976 until 1984, chairman from 1984 until January 1993 and since then chairman emeritus, he has provided continuity in Air Canada's executive suite. "Chairman emeritus" is not a titular role; Taylor averages three days a week at the company, concentrating on its investment in Continental Airlines.

While Taylor began the enormous task of restoring morale at Air Canada and improving customer service, relations between PWA's Don Watson and the Alberta government reached the breaking point in 1976. Although Lougheed had vowed hands off, the vow was not kept. "The government was unable to meet its verbal commitments about no interference and no changes," Watson says. "I didn't understand why it made such commitments because why do people buy a company unless they feel they can do better with it?"

Watson also was concerned that PWA was developing a Crown corporation mentality, just as critics had charged for years had happened at Air Canada. "Employees came to have a false sense of comfort," Watson recalls. "Funding comes too easily to a Crown corporation because banks are unwilling to reject loan requests for fear of an angry government retaliating by withdrawing other business. Whenever money comes easily, there are always employees who can figure how to use it, and eventually expenses come to outstrip earnings."

The showdown between Watson and the Alberta government occurred over Alberta transport minister Hugh Horner's order that PWA move its headquarters from Vancouver to Calgary. His reason was that Calgary "is of increasing importance as the financial centre of Western Canada." Considering that PWA had almost twice as many employees in British Columbia than in Alberta, Watson strongly opposed the move as an unnecessary expense.

"Commuting between Vancouver and Calgary to run the disjointed operation had been expensive and it cost $5 million more to move to Calgary," he points out. "Spending money for purposes other than the benefit of shareholders seemed to me to be a violation of business principles." When he refused to obey the order to move, he was ousted.

PWA needed a new president instantly, providing a leap to the top for a young executive who had already risen rapidly – forty-one-year-old Rhys Eyton. From his standpoint the timing was fortunate because, coincidentally, he had been weighing offers to be president from other companies. He was vacationing in Mexico, deliberating about his future, when he received a telephone call to return immediately to assume PWA's presidency.

Born in Vancouver, Eyton was the son of an automobile executive who died when Eyton was nineteen. Eyton studied business administration at the University of Western Ontario and began his career as a chartered accountant. In 1967 he was working for Vancouver's largest accounting firm when he met PWA's chairman, Bruce Samis, in an elevator. They had known each other casually because Eyton had attended the same high school as Samis's son. By the time the elevator ride ended, Samis had offered Eyton a job, saying PWA needed young men like him. Although Eyton had more lucrative offers from lumber companies, he decided to accept, notwithstanding PWA's then being a small company of about $15 million in revenue. "It's always more fun to get in at the bottom when things aren't certain," Eyton later recalled, contradicting the conventional theory that accountants avoid risk.

Eyton moved upwards quickly at PWA. After a year as assistant to the senior vice-president, finance, he was promoted to manager of PWA's northern operations based in Edmonton. By 1970 he was the region's vice-president. In 1976 he returned to PWA's Vancouver headquarters as executive vice-president, finance. Nine months later he was appointed to succeed Watson. Unlike Watson, Eyton did not oppose PWA's move to Calgary. "You go where the job is," he said. Lougheed says: "We saw Eyton's potential and we were right. He made sure that the airline was run profitably."

How do Taylor and Eyton compare? Taylor is ten years older. He was born in Eastern Canada and Eyton in the West. Both have middle-class backgrounds and live unpretentiously, Taylor near Montreal's Dorval Airport and Eyton overlooking Calgary's Elbow River. Taylor, who is good at remembering employees' names, is regarded by them as being warm and engaging. People differ about Eyton's remembering names, and he is said to be more reserved.

Taylor has spent his entire career at Air Canada; Eyton, most of his at PWA. Both are accountants. Neither is a swashbuckling personality like Grant McConachie and Russell Baker. Both began at their companies in their early years; Eyton became president after nine years, Taylor after twenty. Both were responsible for their companies' privatization from Crown corporations, and undertook major acquisitions. Both were in charge when revenues and profits reached all-time highs; then revenues levelled off and losses mounted to record levels. During their regimes the blood feud between their airlines has been fiercest. In short, their performances are parallel in many ways.

Not only did Air Canada and PWA change presidents in 1976; so did CP Air (as Canadian Pacific Airlines had been renamed in 1968). But its change was occasioned by Gilmore's retirement rather than executive-suite turmoil. His successor was Ian Gray who had joined CP Air one year after its 1942 establishment and four days after graduating as an aeronautical engineer from the University of Detroit across the border from his home town of Windsor, Ontario. He had gone to the Jesuit-operated university because it sponsored his first year's tuition and provided final-year students alternate months in school and industry. CP's airline was a natural choice for Gray because his father had worked for its railway. When he started, Canadian Pacific Airlines had five hundred employees but only one other graduate aeronautical engineer. "The person who interviewed me said, 'You're as green as grass but come on out,'" Gray recalls.

As Gray, Eyton and Taylor settled into their presidencies, the federal government was preparing to dramatically change some of the rules governing the airline industry. Air Canada's "Barbados villa" episode had galvanized public pressure for greater accountability on the part of this Crown corporation. Taxpayers also were concerned that Air Canada benefited from special concessions as the "chosen instrument" of government air policy, yet only had to meet broad objectives under the 1937 Trans-Canada Air Lines Act. These objectives were mostly to "establish, operate and maintain air lines or regular services of aircraft of all kinds" and "to carry on its business throughout Canada or outside of Canada." Although Gordon McGregor, TCA's first president, said that C.D. Howe had told him "to stay out of the taxpayer's pocket," there was no stipulation in the Act that the airline be run as a profitable commercial entity.

Otto Lang, who had fired Air Canada chairman Yves Pratte shortly after becoming minister of transport in 1975, was determined that Air Canada "operate on commercial principles. The old structure had been around for a long time and did not meet the current scene." A Rhodes Scholar who had become a lawyer and Dean of Law at the University of Saskatchewan before being elected to Parliament, Lang believed that Crown corporations "should be run essentially as commercial operations and that any government policy should be included in their operations only as it might with any other commercial entity."

In view of today's events, it is interesting to note that Lang's executive assistant was Peter Wallis, now vice-president, government and regulatory affairs at Canadian Airlines International. As mentioned earlier, Sandy Morrison, Wallis's counterpart at Air Canada, was Jack Pickersgill's executive assistant when Pickersgill was minister of transport.

To achieve his goal of Air Canada "operating on commercial principles," Lang drew up a new Act covering Air Canada. The 1977 Air Canada Act severed the airline's forty-year tie with Canadian National, reorganized its financial structure, placed it under the same licensing procedures as privately-owned carriers, and directed it to "have due regard to sound business principles and, in particular, the contemplation of profit." Lang says Claude Taylor was "enthused" because Air Canada's being a CN subsidiary "no longer made sense – it was an historic accident." Lang believed the public would be better informed as a result. "I believe it is essentially wrong for government policy to develop in a quiet, unknown way. Instead, it should be explicit and clear," he maintains.

It had been Lang's intention to sell some shares in Air Canada to the public –a partial privatization – "to underline that it was to operate on a commercial basis and that it was not carrying a hidden government policy agenda." He believed such a step would force its board "to honour the commercial decisions of management rather than the policy decisions of government."

However, Lang' s plan was thwarted by a fellow Cabinet member whose name Lang refuses to divulge. This Cabinet minister believed the government's veto power over the airline would be diluted by partial privatization. The government had the ultimate decision-making power over Air Canada because the Cabinet controlled appointments and dismissals of directors and senior officials; in addition, budgets required Cabinet and Parliamentary approval.

Nonetheless, as Lang says, "While the speed of privatization was deflected, that was the direction being moved towards." Certainly, Claude Taylor understood this. He immediately began working on a plan for Air Canada's privatization, which was achieved in 1988 and 1989.

* * *

Today, Air Canada and PWA are bitter opponents, but back in 1978 they struck a mutually beneficial agreement when each wanted to buy a regional airline. PWA's target was Transair, the Winnipeg-based regional which had almost acquired PWA in 1961 when PWA's then-president Karl Springer had tried to sell his shares secretly to it. Air Canada wanted to buy Nordair which flew from Montreal into southwestern Ontario and also to Resolute Bay on Cornwallis Island in the far north.

Initially, Air Canada joined CP Air in protesting to the federal government, which had the final say over routes, that PWA's acquisition of Transair would convert PWA from a regional into a potential transcontinental carrier because Transair flew Winnipeg-Dryden-Sault Ste. Marie-Toronto. But subsequently, Air Canada and PWA reached an agreement whereby PWA relinquished the Winnipeg-Toronto route to Air Canada which passed it on to Nordair. In return, Air Canada gave up some of its Winnipeg-Saskatoon and Winnipeg-Regina flights to PWA.

It was a 1978 version of the 1958 arrangement between Canadian Pacific Airlines' Grant McConachie and PWA's Russell Baker whereby Baker withdrew his transcontinental application to support McConachie's in return for Canadian Pacific Airlines' lucrative northwestern routes. As in 1958, PWA decided in 1978 it was more advantageous to increase its regional strength rather than be a third competitor in the tough transcontinental market.

Important as these acquisitions were to Air Canada and PWA, the event that was of paramount importance in 1978 to Canada's airline industry occurred in the United States. That was the year the U.S. Congress passed the Airline Deregulation Act with the backing of the Carter administration. The Act abolished regulation over air fares as well as over entry into and exit from markets.

Eventually, deregulation would come to be seen as a mixed blessing since there were many negative consequences – bankruptcies, labour strife, depressed wages and the termination of service to a number of smaller communities. But, at the outset, public reaction was euphoric. Entrepreneurs grabbed the opportunity to start their own airline and consumers were thrilled at fare reductions.

The open market in the United States gave impetus to CP Air's campaign for the Canadian government to award it a greater market share. In 1977, Lang had permitted it to increase its share to 35 percent from the 25 percent Pickersgill had allowed. Each year, to quantify that share, Air Canada and CP Air supplied annual traffic forecasts to the government which had the final say. To ensure Ottawa's giving CP Air "its fair share," CP Air's president, Ian Gray, flew there every two weeks.

In 1979, CP Air got even more than it had sought when just three days before Parliament was dissolved for an election, Lang announced that it would no longer be tied to a fixed share of the transcontinental market. For CP Air, it was the culmination of a long battle fought by three presidents – McConachie, Gilmore and Gray – covering a period of more than thirty years. Mackenzie King's edict that Trans-Canada Air Lines was to be "the sole Canadian agency" in international and transcontinental flights was dead.

The end of Air Canada's transcontinental monopoly did not mean wide open competition existed across Canada. Instead of a monopoly, there was now a duopoly – a duopoly that has continued to the present. Indeed, Lang's principal objective was to keep the regionals "from going into the national business." To him, the restriction made sound economic sense. "It's very expensive to have multiple airlines serving particular points. They all must have ground crews, check-in counters, more planes, more pilots, and so on, and there is a limit to how many airlines even major markets can support," he explains.

The carnage that resulted in the deregulated U.S. market bears him out. Most of the new carriers formed to cash in on the anticipated gold mine there no longer exist because supply far exceeded demand. Sixteen U.S. airlines have been absorbed by others. Of the ten large carriers that continue to operate, two –America West, the sole surviving airline that came into existence after U.S. deregulation started, and Trans World Airlines – are under bankruptcy protection. Air Canada invested in Continental, the fifth-largest, when it emerged from bankruptcy protection in 1993. The remaining airlines – Alaska, American, Delta, Northwest, Southwest, United and US Air – are battling in a mature market surfeited with seat capacity.

From 1990 until the end of 1992, the U.S. airline industry lost U.S.$11 billion. Only Southwest, a no-frills, low-fare, low-cost, short-haul carrier made a profit in 1992. AMR Corporation, American's parent, which agreed in 1992 to invest $246 million in Canadian Airlines International, lost U.S.$25 million that year, compared to a $5 million profit in 1991. But the other two major U.S. airlines fared far worse. United Airlines lost U.S.$538 million in 1992 and $494 million in 1991; Delta, $822 million and $275 million.

By the late 1980s, Lang had changed his opinion about the merits of two transcontinental airlines. "I came to the conclusion that due to the increased financial difficulties of the airlines and the recession that Canada could only sustain one airline," he says. In 1991, as Air Canada's and PWA's financial situations deteriorated, Lang publicly suggested that the Mulroney government "give its blessing" to a merger. "One strong profitable airline makes more sense than two in trouble and competition from foreign carriers would still be strenuous on international routes," he says.

As for CP Air, its victory bears out the saying, "Be careful what you want because you may get it." CP Air did want to go from a 35 percent to a 40 percent share of the transcontinental market. That increase would have meant a manageable hike in expenditures since it was only 5 percent more than the share CP Air already had. But the total removal of market share restrictions forced CP Air to spend an enormous $1 billion on a fleet expansion program, rent more ticket counter space at airports, and build a new hangar in Toronto.

Naturally, it could not order planes ahead of time based merely on conjecture that Lang would lift the barrier. Unfortunately, delivery of the planes coincided with rising fuel prices and interest rates as well as the 1982 recession which caused a severe decline in passenger travel. Because it takes two years to build a plane, it is a common misfortune in the airline industry to order planes in good times and to take delivery in bad times.

CP Air could have decided not to engage in all-out competition against Air Canada, but such a decision would have conflicted with its entire history. "We had to put up or shut up. There was no way we could back out unless we had been merely shooting the breeze for almost forty years," Gray says.

Therefore, CP Air "put up," although there was no immediate impact on the distribution of travel between it and Air Canada due to the time it took for CP Air to get more planes and the subsequent recession. But an important transformation had occurred in Canadian aviation. The concept of a "privileged airline" was dead and duopoly had arrived. For Air Canada, there no longer was any advantage to being state-owned, thereby setting the stage for its privatization.

While the industry coped with executive turnover and regulation changes in the 1970s, passenger travel boomed, more than doubling by 1980 to 28 million trips. During the same period, air freight volume increased by more than 100 million kilograms.

Consequently, the outlook seemed excellent and the airlines responded optimistically with years of exuberant expansion. Based on past growth increases in traffic and financial results, their optimism was understandable. But they failed to take into account the most basic of economic facts – good times do not last forever.

CHAPTER THREE

The Years of Rapid Change (1980 –1985)

During the 1980s, Canada's airlines underwent more change than in all their previous history, with mixed results for them, their investors and the travelling public. CP Air aggressively overhauled its route system and marketing thrust. It also acquired three eastern regional carriers – Eastern Provincial Airways, Nordair and Quebecair. CP Air was then bought by Pacific Western Airlines which went on to take over Wardair, Canada's third-largest airline and leading charter operator. These purchases catapulted PWA from a regional carrier into Canada's second-largest national and international airline.

Also during this decade of rapid change, Air Canada and PWA were privatized and government regulation of routes and fares ended in the hope that increased competition would result in more choice and lower fares for the consumer through permitting all carriers – national, regional and local – to enter any domestic market. Fares did drop, but instead of creating more choice, deregulation intensified industry consolidation as it prompted Air Canada and PWA to establish or buy regional feeder affiliates across the country (and PWA to also acquire Wardair). Thus, these years of acquisitions, consolidation, privatization and deregulation completely transformed Canada's airline industry. Yet, the end result was a duopoly, as had been the case when the decade began – only now it consisted of Air Canada and PWA rather than Air Canada and CP Air. Many developments overlapped and influenced one another. Here is a summary of these events; the details follow.

CP Air began to overhaul its route system and marketing in 1982. PWA was privatized in 1983. In 1984, PWA acquired a large minority interest in March in Time Air, a regional airline serving Alberta and British Columbia. In April, CP Air bought Eastern Provincial Airways, and in May, the federal government of Pierre Trudeau unveiled plans for deregulation. In June, Air Canada got a new president when the eight-year incumbent,

Claude Taylor, stepped up to the chairmanship; and in September, the Conservatives under Brian Mulroney defeated the Liberals.

In March 1985, CP Air got a new president; in July, the Tories' deregulation program was introduced; and in November, CP Air made a takeover offer for Nordair. In June 1986, the first reading of the Tories' deregulation legislation was given; a Nordair affiliate acquired Quebecair in August; and PWA made its offer to purchase CP Air in December.

The year 1987 was crammed even more with events. In January, Air Canada bought 75 percent of the Air Ontario regional airline. At the beginning of February, PWA's takeover of CP Air was finalized. Later that month, Air Canada acquired 100 percent of AirBC, a British Columbia regional airline. In April, PWA merged its operations and CP Air's under the name Canadian Airlines International Limited (CAIL). In July, Air Canada and PWA formed a jointly owned computer reservation system called The Gemini Group Automated Distribution System. (Gemini was to be the source of much of the friction in 1992 and 1993 between Air Canada and PWA when PWA wanted to withdraw in compliance with AMR Corporation's demand that it do so and then join AMR's computer reservation system in return for AMR's making a substantial investment in Canadian Airlines.)

Later in that same month of July 1987, Ontario Express, a regional affiliate created by PWA, started operations, and PWA acquired 45 percent of Calm Air International, a Manitoba airline that flies to northern Manitoba and the Northwest Territories. In September, PWA established Inter-Canadien, a Quebec regional carrier.

The next year, 1988, began with the National Transportation Act 1987 coming into effect on January 1. This milestone legislation stipulated that market forces, rather than economic regulation, should govern the supply of air services. It brought to an end close to a half-century of government regulation over prices and routes that had begun with the formation of the Air Transport Board in 1944 by the Mackenzie King government, seven years after it had created Air Canada under the name Trans-Canada Air Lines. In March, Air Canada founded Air Alliance, a Quebec regional carrier; in May, it acquired Northwest Territorial Airways and, in September, its privatization was set in motion when the government sold 43 percent of its shares to the public.

The decade ended with PWA's acquisition of Wardair in April 1989 and the completion of Air Canada's privatization in July.

Many of the changes in the 1980s were sparked by the airlines' plunge from the glory days of the 1970s into financial disarray. The acquisitions were largely a matter of the strong gobbling up the weak, or the less weak the weaker. Deregulation was partly prompted by the government's wanting to avoid bailing out Air Canada which was in trouble, notwithstanding regulation that protected its position as the dominant national airline.

Although the industry worldwide entered the 1980s confident that the 1970s boom would continue, by 1982 it was in distress due to an enormous jump in fuel costs and interest rates, and the resulting economic crisis, by far the worst since the 1930s, caused a sharp decline in passenger travel. When the Organization of Petroleum Exporting Countries (OPEC) sharply increased its oil prices, fuel costs as a percentage of Canadian airlines' expenses climbed from 19.8 percent in 1979 to 22.2 percent in 1980, 25.3 percent in 1981, and 25.1 percent in 1982. Over and above these industry-wide woes, CP Air had an additional problem – the steep cost of buying new planes to maintain an equal footing with Air Canada following the federal government's termination of Air Canada's monopoly in 1979. All of these difficulties caused CP Air to suffer a 1981 loss of $23 million and a much steeper one of $39 million in 1982.

This near doubling of losses came in conjunction with the retirement of Ian Gray as CP Air's president after holding the position for eight years. In its fifty years the airline had had only four presidents – W.M. Neal, Grant McConachie, Jack Gilmore and Gray – and all were from within the company or its parent, Canadian Pacific. But, in 1982, a break was made from this tradition with the importation of an outsider – Daniel Colussy, a fifty-one-year-old American with extensive experience in all aspects of running an airline. He had been director of operations at American Airlines and marketing vice-president at Northeast Airlines. He was also in charge of passenger marketing at Pan American and then president of that airline from 1978 to 1980.

CP Air's need for a new president coincided with Colussy's sudden one for a new job. He had left Pan Am in 1980 in order to start his own airline. It was his misfortune that just as he was due to begin operations, U.S. air traffic controllers went on strike effectively killing his venture. One month later an executive search firm approached him about the CP Air job. Although he was aware that CP Air was in trouble, Colussy accepted the presidency since he believed the airline had many strengths. "It was well regarded by the business community because it was a private, rather than government airline, and its international network spanned five continents and was doing well," he says.

He also believed that what he regarded as CP Air's greatest weakness – its Canadian route structure – could be readily corrected. "The domestic market was not well organized in that there was no feed of traffic within the system and little access to Eastern Canada," he recalls. "Also, planes designed for long-range international flights were wrongly assigned to short-haul domestic flights."

To increase traffic feed, Colussy introduced to Canada the hub-and-spoke system already prevalent in the United States. Under this system, passengers from various places – the spokes – fly into a centralized airport – the hub – and then continue on to their destination on connecting flights to other hubs and spokes. So as to maximize this feed, as many flights as possible are scheduled to arrive around the same time at hubs from spokes. For CP Air, the system offered an additional advantage; it would enable it to increase its transcontinental market share, now that the federal government had ended Air Canada's monopoly.

Previously, Vancouver was CP Air's focal point as a gateway to both the Pacific Rim and the interior of British Columbia. Colussy decided to develop Toronto as a central Canada hub to also include incoming passengers from the United States with ultimate destinations elsewhere in Canada. This decision meant CP Air would be battling Air Canada head-on in Toronto, Air Canada's major market. Therefore, before undertaking his plan Colussy requested a meeting with Air Canada's president, Claude Taylor, at Air Canada's Montreal headquarters "to get the lay of the land." Specifically, Colussy wondered if Taylor would be agreeable to a small joint reduction in flights so as to increase the number of seats filled on the remaining flights and thereby maintain profit levels.

Considering that both Air Canada's and Canadian Airlines International's current troubles are largely due to overcapacity for which each holds the other primarily responsible, Colussy was well ahead of his time. Taylor, who is well regarded for his pleasant manners, received him courteously, but rejected his suggestion. "Claude Taylor was too much of a gentleman to throw me out, but he did say he was happy with his system and saw no need to change. If I had been in his place, I would have done the same," Colussy recollects.

Having received the response he expected, Colussy returned to CP Air's Vancouver headquarters and "cranked up our operation." He totally revamped CP Air's flight schedule so as to make Toronto the central connecting point. In addition, he developed a cooperative agreement in 1983 with Eastern Provincial Airways for quick, convenient connections, thereby creating through-service between Western Canada and Halifax since EPA flew the Toronto-Halifax route and CP Air did not. Colussy also obtained interline exchanges with a number of U.S. airlines, particularly US Air, whereby each fed traffic to the other at Toronto.

The CP Air-Eastern Provincial cooperative agreement came just three years after a bitter dispute between them over the Toronto-Halifax route.

As Air Canada flew the route, CP Air wanted it, too, to be on a truly equal basis as a transcontinental airline. For its part, EPA, then a regional airline serving the Atlantic provinces, maintained that the profitable Toronto-Halifax run would help it make up losses from money-losing local flights. CP Air was supported by the Halifax Board of Trade, the Nova Scotia Tourist Industry Association, and local exporters and importers who believed CP Air's national and international service would be helpful in attracting business from across Canada and the world.

The Canadian Transport Commission awarded the route to CP Air, but EPA fought on by lining up support from the Atlantic premiers. They sent telegrams to Prime Minister Trudeau, pleading that the Cabinet reverse the CTC's decision. Their lobbying worked. Just ten days before CP's inaugural Toronto-Halifax flights, the Cabinet revoked the CTC's decision and gave the route to EPA, at the same time cancelling EPA's Montreal-Halifax route. Subsequently, CP Air launched a Montreal-Halifax route which it yielded to EPA as part of their 1983 agreement.

Shortly after EPA won the Toronto-Halifax route, its owner and president Harry Steele proposed to CP Air's then-president Ian Gray that CP Air buy its airline. The two men went to see CP chairman Ian Sinclair whose reaction was pungent. When Gray went in first to make the suggestion, "Ian told me, in effect, to get lost," Gray recalls. "He refused to see Steele." His anger was understandable taking into account how EPA had just managed to get the awarding of the Toronto-Halifax route to CP Air revoked. But Sinclair was not so irate that he ruled out ever acquiring EPA. "Wait until EPA gets into trouble," he advised Gray. CP Air only had to wait two years.

While CP Air bided its time to buy EPA, Colussy purchased CP's hotel division in December 1983 on the premise that the airline and the hotels would feed each other business, as he had seen happen between Pan Am, his former employer, and its hotel subsidiary. His prediction came true. The hotels did boost CP Air's financial performance significantly. In 1984, it had its strongest financial results in years – a profit of $9 million compared to combined losses of $64 million between 1981 and 1983. Two-thirds of that profit was made by CP Hotels.

Bearing in mind what he saw as CP Air's strength – the empathy of businesspeople towards an airline that also was private enterprise – Colussy decided to develop a distinctive niche for CP Air as the business traveller's airline, rather than compete against Air Canada for every customer. For many years businesspeople who travelled on tickets which cost more than twice as much as discounted tickets used primarily by vacationers, had complained that their expensive tickets gave them no benefits other than penalty exemption if they changed flight bookings. Finally, in 1978, KLM

Royal Dutch Airlines became the first airline to try to make these travellers happier by providing separate business-class cabins, better food than for "economy" passengers, free beverages, and free headphones for inflight entertainment. However, roomier seats were not provided; thus it remained impossible for business travellers to spread out their work comfortably.

Prior to Colussy's arrival, CP Air had begun business-class service on a limited basis under then-president Ian Gray. But, like other airlines, CP Air did not change the seating arrangement which requires modified cabin interiors and specially designed seats. Colussy decided to spend on these improvements, introducing greater seat room first on international flights and after a year, on domestic flights. The service was aggressively marketed under the name "Attaché" business class to emphasize the space now available for working from attaché cases.

While spending on upgraded service for passengers, Colussy undertook considerable organizational cost-cutting as a counterbalancing measure. Upon his arrival, he laid off more than one thousand employees and closed the three hiring offices in Vancouver, Toronto and Montreal for six weeks "to make my point that it was essential to hold down the head count."

While Colussy was making his dynamic imprint on CP Air, important changes were occurring at PWA. In December 1983, the same month that Colussy bought CP Hotels, the Alberta government, in a smooth transaction, privatized PWA after nine years of ownership. Wide public ownership was ensured by limiting individual shareholdings to a maximum of 10 percent.

Outside of appointing additional businesspeople to PWA's board "to strengthen it," the Alberta government under Peter Lougheed had left operational matters to PWA's management. Nor had it put in additional money. By 1983, only one of Lougheed's objectives in buying PWA had been fully realized – that of developing Alberta as an important regional centre. Air freight of agricultural products had not done well; Lougheed says the idea was "premature." The third goal of helping Alberta become the gateway to the North was hampered by sluggish economic activity in the Territories.

Lougheed decided December 1983 was a suitable time to sell for several reasons. He wanted to honour his assurance to his Conservative Party that he would privatize PWA and he wished to do so well in advance of his planned 1985 retirement from politics. Because PWA, unlike Canada's other airlines, had been profitable in 1982, Lougheed was able to sell it at a considerable profit. After leaving politics, he joined the Calgary law firm of Bennett Jones Verchere which had represented PWA for years, but he did not act on any PWA legal matters. In 1989, he became a member of PWA's board of directors.

The privatization set the stage for PWA's expansion in the following years because it provided it with a pool of capital. President Rhys Eyton believed the time had came to look for growth opportunities. He and his managers vaguely considered diversification into non-airline businesses, bearing in mind that during the 1970s Eyton had been assigned to turn around a money-losing trucking company owned by PWA.

The diversification idea faded away when Eyton chose instead to buy the type of business with which PWA was more familiar – a regional airline. His target was Time Air, a highly successful carrier in Alberta and British Columbia. Time Air had been established in 1966 in Lethbridge, Alberta under the name Lethbridge Air Service by Walter Rodney "Stubb" Ross who started with a small plane and was ticket agent, pilot and chauffeur. He would pick up customers before dawn at their homes in his Volkswagen bus, drive them to the Lethbridge airport, and then fly them to Calgary. He changed his company's name to Time Air in 1970 when he expanded to Red Deer and Edmonton.

In 1982, the federal government awarded Time Air the Lethbridge-Vancouver route. It turned out to be highly popular with Japanese visitors to Canada because Lethbridge had a large Japanese population. All told, by 1984 Time Air had grown to fifty-two flights to ten communities in Alberta and British Columbia, including the busy Lethbridge-Calgary one which PWA had coveted for years.

Thus, in March 1984 PWA began its expansion by buying just under 50 percent of Time Air. In so doing, it was buying into a success for a modest sum – $4.3 million. It integrated Time Air's schedules with its own, thereby feeding traffic into its own system and strengthening its position as Canada's leading regional airline. Ross died in 1987, and in 1991 PWA acquired the rest of Time Air.

In April 1984, CP Air was able to act on CP chairman Ian Sinclair's 1982 advice to wait until Eastern Provincial Airways was in trouble before making a takeover offer. EPA's troubles began in January 1983 when the company locked out mechanics and clerical staff. One week later, the pilots walked off in sympathy. A bitter six-month strike followed, and as a result EPA was unprofitable in 1983.

Owing to its weak position, CP Air was able to pay much less than it would have had to in 1982. The takeover strengthened CP Air's hub-and-spoke system because EPA's Maritime routes fed traffic into CP Air's Toronto hub. Also, CP Air was able to begin a Halifax-Amsterdam service.

* * *

While all these changes were taking place, the movement toward deregulation of the industry was gaining momentum. Since the industry's earliest days, the federal government had decreed which airline could fly what routes, what equipment it could use, and what prices it could charge. Regulation had been the government's method of ensuring the airlines' survival and of providing equal service across Canada. But by the 1980s, it was questionable whether these objectives were being met.

Regulation had failed to provide equal access across Canada by the government-owned airline, Air Canada. By 1984, it served only four communities with populations under twenty-five thousand out of the many such places in the country. Nor had protection against competition brought the industry much financial security. In 1982, PWA was the only profitable major airline. Otherwise, industry losses totalled a staggering $83 million. Air Canada had suffered 19 percent of that loss – $15.8 million – and it also had a high debt-equity ratio owing to recent extensive aircraft purchases to update its fleet. The government did not want to have to bail out Air Canada with an equity infusion of taxpayers' money.

Also, Canadians were continuing to urge the government to deregulate air fares so that they could enjoy the type of deep discounts available in the United States following the deregulation of the airline industry there in 1978. Although the Canadian government had subsequently forced Canada's airlines to offer discounts of up to 35 percent, few Canadians were able to take advantage of them because not many of these seats were offered per flight and they were subject to lengthy advanced booking requirements.

The restrictions displeased the airlines' two main constituencies. Leisure travellers were annoyed at the limited number of seats available. Business travellers regarded the fares as discriminatory. They resented the fact that leisure travellers who could reserve their seats in advance and were willing to stay at their destination over a Saturday night before returning were travelling on the same plane for much less. Although the airlines served businesspeople free liquor, they were not placated because the value of the drinks was by no means equivalent to the difference between their full fares and the discount rates. Both groups became even more upset when the airlines raised all fares in an effort to restore profitability after the damaging impact of the 1982 recession on their financial performance.

Businesspeople were further annoyed that their counterparts in the United States were paying lower fares on the new discount airlines that had sprung up after deregulation. Although fares on the established major U.S. airlines were still higher than Canadian fares when converted to Canadian dollars, U.S. business travellers had the choice of flying on discount carriers.

In order to take advantage of fares to places within the United States as well as to overseas that were considerably lower than what Canadian carriers charged to those destinations, many Canadians living near the border went by car or bus to nearby U.S. airports. A Gallup poll estimated that 11 percent of Canadians travelling by plane began their flights in the United States. Their doing so contributed to air passenger traffic in the United States rising by 20.9 percent between 1978, the year deregulation began there, and 1982. The comparative figure for Canada was only 2.4 percent.

But in their envy of the lower fares and more choice that deregulation had brought in the United States, Canadians overlooked the many drawbacks. They included inequality in fares between highly and less travelled routes, an industry shakeout, and the layoffs of thousands of airline employees.

Fares did drop spectacularly on busy American routes; for instance, a one-way fare between New York and Los Angeles (2,475 miles) cost just $119, and between Dallas and Houston (217 miles) only $25. But fares remained high on lightly travelled routes; for example, the fare one-way from Denver to North Platte, Nebraska (207 miles) was $163 – six and a half times the rate from Dallas to Houston, about the same distance. Deregulation had generated greater competition only on the more widely travelled routes.

Moreover, service had deteriorated. In the hope of increasing their revenue, the airlines scheduled more flights at peak hours than airports could handle. According to a survey on the impact of overscheduling, nine out of ten U.S. frequent fliers (those flying at least three times a year) had been on late departing or arriving flights. One out of five had been delayed for longer than four hours; 45 percent had had their flights cancelled; and 22 percent had been bumped from flights because of overbooking. In addition, the airlines concentrated on serving bigger communities to the dismay of the smaller centres where service was either sharply reduced or terminated.

Also, the chief attraction of deregulation for Americans – cheaper fares – was shortlived. A comparison of 1978 and 1984 fares between seventy U.S. cities found that in three out of five cases they had increased by at least 80 percent, whereas the Consumer Price Index for the same period had risen much less – 36 percent. The deep discount fares had quickly vanished because the "no frills" carriers went bankrupt or were bought by bigger airlines. As one critic bitingly put it, "Deregulation in the United States has created a few low fares for a few people, to a few places, sometimes, for awhile."

U.S. deregulation also failed to weaken the grip of the dominant airlines on the industry. Instead, it strengthened markedly. The top ten airlines' market share soared from 89.7 percent in 1970, eight years prior to deregulation, to 93.9 percent in 1986. Thus, most U.S. travellers had lost rather than profited from deregulation.

The gains of the ten airlines contrasted to the mergers or bankruptcies of many others which had been unable to survive the squeeze between decreased revenue, due to the lower fares, and continuing high costs. Although the discount fares did increase overall traffic, the increase was insufficient to support all the existing and new airlines. In their search for lower costs which the economic pressures of deregulation forced upon them, the surviving airlines had few options because such costs as fuel, air navigation services, landing fees and interest rates are set by the government and are undifferentiated between carriers. Labour costs are one of the few items under an airline's control, and in the U.S., airline employees had borne the brunt of the airlines' cost-cutting efforts. Canadian workers feared that the same would happen to them.

The U.S. airlines had maintained that through limiting the entry of new companies into the industry, government regulation had resulted in the unions becoming too powerful. By negotiating with each airline in turn, they were sometimes able to "whip-saw" the entire industry into granting additional pay or work-rule concessions. Moreover, when rivalry between companies was particularly bitter, it was a regular practice for one company to make a work-rule concession which would not hurt it much, but would greatly harm its competitor when it was forced to agree to the same terms.

The wage and work-rule concessions were not too damaging to the airlines' balance sheets while the introduction of faster and larger aircraft increased overall worker productivity. But, by the 1980s, major aircraft productivity increases had reached a plateau. Thus, the airlines insisted that worker concessions were essential for the companies' survival. These concessions amounted to hundreds of millions of dollars in pay cuts, wage freezes and deferral of increases. Two-tier wage scales were established whereby newer employees were paid as much as 50 percent less for the same work. Higher-paid employees were encouraged to leave through early retirement programs; this enabled the airlines to hire replacements at the lower-tier wages. Vacation, holiday, overtime and sick leave entitlements as well as medical and dental benefits were reduced. Moreover, in addition to these cutbacks, the U.S. airlines had laid off fifty thousand workers – more than the total forty-two thousand employed in the entire Canadian airline industry.

But, when Lloyd Axworthy became Trudeau's minister of transport in 1983, Canadians generally were unaware of how deregulation had made U.S. air service poorer and that many fare decreases soon were reversed. Nor were they concerned about the potential hardships for the airlines and their employees. They simply wanted to pay less, just like they thought Americans were. "It was clearly foolish to think that we could continue a protectionist policy in view of deregulation in the United States," Axworthy says. "The question was what adjustments to make."

In his opinion, Canadian governments throughout the years were as much to blame as the airlines for the industry's problems because they "had offered little comprehensive policy direction since the passage of the 1967 National Transportation Act." Axworthy further thought that for too long civil servants, rather than elected politicians, had set policy, a charge that politicians often make about the power struggle between themselves and the bureaucrats as to who knows best. Moreover, he believed that senior civil servants had developed "too strong an identity of interests" with the airline industry because they were in frequent contact with the presidents of the various airlines through meetings of the Air Transport Association of Canada. In addition, airline representatives were present at government-to-government negotiations for bilateral air agreements between Canada and other countries.

Axworthy says that this cosy relationship led the civil servants to side with the airlines' opposition to deregulation. Looking back on his struggle with his own department, he adds: "The department was drinking its own bathwater and didn't like a minister setting directions for it." Thus, when Axworthy argued the merits of deregulation, department officials echoed the airlines' argument that "The Canadian market, thinly populated and strung out along the border, was very different from that of the United States. They also maintained that Canadian carriers were far too fragile to tolerate competition."

Axworthy was supported by the department's most senior civil servant – his deputy minister. However, he was only one person out of many. There-fore, Axworthy decided that he could succeed only by circumventing the Civil Service. He did so by establishing a policy unit supporting his views within his own office. It consisted of an official seconded from the Privy Council Office, one of Axworthy's assistants, a consumer advocacy lawyer retained as counsel, and several academics. Additionally, Axworthy set up an interdepartmental task force with representatives from the Departments of Labour, Finance, and Consumer and Corporate Affairs as well as the Treasury Board at which he encouraged consumer representatives to par-ticipate. To underline his commitment to public debate, he appointed a special counsel to represent the public interest, the first time this had been done.

Axworthy's critics, however, maintained that he was creating an unnec-essary political confrontation with the Canadian Transport Commission, especially after his office made public a letter he had sent the Commission's president, saying the government would force the Commission to comply with his program should the Commission attempt to resist it. From the time the CTC was established, ministers of transport had complained that the CTC's president, in effect, was a second minister of transport, a situation that as one of Axworthy's predecessors, George Hees, put it, was "unworkable."

The result of all this manoeuvring was the "New Canadian Air Policy," which Axworthy announced in May 1984. Its basic elements were less regulation and more competition through the abolition of the distinct roles of national, regional and local carriers, thereby allowing any carrier to apply for any route and to use any type of equipment. The plan also called for the elimination of government fare price controls in two years' time.

The New Canadian Air Policy was never taken to the next step and drafted as legislation because its introduction coincided with the last days of the Liberal government. One month after it was unveiled, the Liberals held a leadership convention for a successor to Trudeau who had retired. Shortly afterward, John Turner, the new prime minister, called an election for September and the Liberals were defeated by the Progressive Conservatives under Brian Mulroney. Although there had been speculation that the Conservatives would slow down the movement towards deregulation, the idea was so popular with the public that they pressed onward.

Between the release of Axworthy's New Canadian Air Policy and the Conservatives coming into power, Air Canada got a new president and chief executive officer in June 1984. In that Claude Taylor, who had held the dual titles for eight years, became chairman and Pierre Jeanniot, who had been executive vice-president and chief operating officer, succeeded Taylor, their appointments appeared to be similar to the normal course of events at a corporation. However, in reality, the situation was not at all routine.

Instead, the government, having decided not to renew Taylor's contract as president and CEO upon its expiration, launched a three-month search for a successor within and without Air Canada before appointing the fifty-one-year-old Jeanniot to the position. Taylor was fifty-nine, six years short of the usual mandatory retirement age of sixty-five. As he was very unhappy over not being reappointed CEO, Jeanniot says he "pleaded with the government to name Taylor chairman on the basis that too many chairmen from outside Air Canada had been appointed in the past." Also in Taylor's favour was the stability which his long tenure had provided the company.

Jeanniot came to regret having made the suggestion because in his view Taylor was "instrumental in building opposition to my plans within Air Canada's board," leading to Jeanniot's quitting in 1990. "Seeing how it turned out, in retrospect I would not do it again," Jeanniot comments regarding Taylor's chairmanship.

In theory, Taylor and Jeanniot should have been a good team. Taylor's background in marketing and Jeanniot's in engineering were complementary, and for several years they had worked well together. Taylor was Canadian by birth and Air Canada was his first and only employer. Jeanniot's route to the airline was more colourful and involved more hardship.

Jeanniot's parents lived in Ethiopia where his father ran a railroad, but he was born in France, in 1933, because his mother preferred to be in a hospital there. His father died when Pierre was thirteen and his mother, who had been visiting a sister in Montreal, decided to remain in Canada with Pierre and her two other children. For ten years Jeanniot undertook a tiring schedule of daytime work and university night classes in engineering and business administration. His first job was as an electrical draftsman at what is now Northern Telecom. After eighteen months, he joined Sperry Gyroscope of Canada, an aviation instrument manufacturer. Its chief engineer was so impressed by Jeanniot that he made him a junior engineer even though he was not much over twenty years old and was still studying for his engineering degree.

It was while he was at Sperry that Jeanniot came to the attention of Air Canada (still known as Trans-Canada Air Lines) in 1955; Sperry was supplying the airline with instruments for a new fleet of planes. Twenty-two at the time, he was hired as part of a small group of quality control technicians whose job was to analyze technical difficulties so as to prevent their recurrence. Next, Jeanniot helped design a computer program that simulated an aircraft engine's life cycle and predicted when it would need to be replaced. He also played a role in developing the "black box," a flight data recorder used in analyzing plane crashes.

During the rest of the 1950s and throughout the 1960s, Jeanniot held various technical positions. In 1970, when thirty-seven, he became Air Canada's first Francophone vice-president, heading the airline's newly created computer and systems department which encompassed telecommunications and technical operational research as well as computer operations. Subsequently, Jeanniot held positions in corporate planning and marketing.

In 1980, Taylor recommended to the government, which had the final say over appointments, that Jeanniot be made executive vice-president and chief of airline operations, and in 1983 he suggested that Jeanniot be promoted to chief operating officer. With Jeanniot in charge of airline operations from 1980 on, Taylor concentrated primarily on Air Canada's external relations. Thus, when Jeanniot replaced Taylor as CEO, it seemed as if their working relationship would continue to be harmonious. But the goodwill was soon dissipated by a power struggle.

While this conflict was building, the industry, public and new Conservative government were concentrating on the vital issue of deregulation.

Mulroney and the Tories placed airline deregulation high on their list of priorities because it fitted in with their overall objective of reducing the government's role in the economy. In addition to the airline industry, Mulroney wanted to deregulate the rest of the transportation sector, plus oil and gas, and financial services. He maintained that deregulation would benefit the public because the increased competitive pressure on companies would force them to cut prices and offer more choice.

Mulroney appointed Donald Mazankowski as transport minister; he had held the position during the brief time Joe Clark had been prime minister five years earlier. His executive assistant then had been Peter Wallis, who had held the same post under Otto Lang when Lang had been minister of transport. (Wallis left government service in 1980 to become staff vice-president, regulatory affairs, at PWA and is now vice-president, government and regulatory affairs at Canadian Airlines International.) "We wanted a more market-oriented approach," Mazankowski says. He believed this approach would not only benefit consumers, but also the airlines, because it would compel them to be "on the leading edge of competitive challenges and of the globalization that was occurring."

Unlike Axworthy, who believed most of the officials in the Transport Department had joined ranks with the airline industry to oppose his reform efforts, Mazankowski says he had "excellent cooperation from the Department and the entire transportation industry. We discussed and debated our proposals in an open and thorough way, indicating that our policy would be an evolution, not a revolution."

In July 1985, Mazankowski released a white paper as the first step towards legislating deregulation. Entitled "Freedom To Move: A Framework for Transportation Reform," the paper was concerned with all aspects of transportation – air, rail, trucking, marine transport and commodity pipelines.

Like the "New Canadian Air Policy," "Freedom To Move" recommended less regulation and more competition. It called for complete deregulation of air fares and for all carriers to have complete freedom to move into any domestic market. International routes are arranged through bilateral agreements between countries.

Based on the disillusioning experience of deregulation in the United States, Canadian airline employees strongly opposed "Freedom To Move," as evidenced in the following excerpt from the submission of the airline division of the Canadian Union of Public Employees, which represents 90 percent of Canada's flight attendants. "We all know the preference of the current Federal Government: free trade and the dominance of market forces," the presentation said. "But as economic history shows, a free-enterprise economy, left to its own unregulated operation, will inevitably produce economic concentration, bankruptcies and instability verging on chaos. The alleged virtues of an economy based on perfect competition have never existed outside of first year university neoclassical economics textbooks."

Besides increasing industry concentration, CUPE maintained that, just as had occurred in the United States, deregulation would lead to "less reliable service, higher average fares, reduced safety, employment loss and dislocation and restricted regional development." Some of these predictions did not materialize. Smaller and medium-sized communities still get service, sometimes on a more frequent basis, albeit by connector airlines owned by Air Canada and PWA, and by smaller planes. Other predictions – a resurgence in fare prices and job layoffs – did become reality. But there is disagreement as to whether deregulation was the cause, a cause, or not a factor at all. Those who do not solely blame deregulation also place the responsibility on the weak economy. They claim the slump forced the airlines to reduce jobs and raise fares so as to improve profits, even though the conventional wisdom is that higher fares cause a decline in passenger travel.

There also is debate over deregulation's impact on air safety. Air Canada and Canadian Airlines International have not had any fatal crashes since deregulation. The worst post-deregulation disaster was the March 10, 1989 crash of an Air Ontario jet at Dryden, Ontario, in which twenty-seven people were killed. Air Ontario was then 75 percent-owned by Air Canada. The cause of the crash was investigated under the federal Inquiries Act by a one-man commission, Justice Virgil Moshansky. While he said inadequate de-icing procedures were largely to blame, he also found deregulation to be a contributory cause because of "the real concerns created by deregulation regarding profitability." He concluded that these concerns led to "Air Canada's management requiring Air Ontario only to comply with Transport Canada's threshold operational safety standards. . . . This resulted in a lower level of flight safety being available to Air Ontario passengers than to Air Canada passengers."

But he emphasized that Transport Canada was equally at fault because it had not been "more diligent." His findings led to a considerable tightening in Canada's air safety standards. But some of his recommendations have not yet been implemented. Also, Transport Canada's emphasis on industry self-policing of safety standards, while in keeping with the government's overall deregulation policy, falls short of Moshansky's call for increased government surveillance and enforcement.

As had happened in the United States, the airlines demanded worker concessions, prompting strikes at six airlines: Air Canada, CP Air, Pacific

Western, Nordair, Eastern Provincial and Air Ontario. Also as had happened in the United States, there was increased competition. Consequently, Canadian travellers obtained what they had sought for so long — broader choice and lower fares.

Major transcontinental routes that previously were the exclusive possession of Air Canada and CP Air could now be served by an additional four to five carriers depending on the route. For example, between Winnipeg and Toronto, they could fly via Air Canada, CP Air, PWA, Nordair or Air Ontario. In addition, far more people were now able to travel on discount fares. In 1985, 53 percent of all passengers on domestic scheduled flights were discount customers compared to only 45 percent in 1983.

But, as had occurred in the United States, the broader choice and deep discounts were shortlived. During the second half of the 1980s, CP Air gained control of two eastern regional airlines — Nordair and Quebecair. Thereupon, PWA bought CP Air and Wardair, replacing CP Air as Canada's second-largest airline. Air Canada and PWA strengthened their duopoly by buying or starting up regional affiliates across Canada. In addition, deregulation was enforced in a new transportation act and Air Canada was privatized. Thus the vast transformation that began in the first half of the 1980s continued unabated during the remainder of the decade.

CHAPTER FOUR

The Changes Continue (1985 – 1989)

1985 and 1986 were CP Air's last hurrah. In bidding for Nordair, a Quebec regional, in November 1985, it was the first major airline to pursue a smaller one in the months following the announcement of the "Freedom To Move" deregulation policy. At the same time it acquired Nordair in August 1986, a Nordair affiliate took over Quebecair, Quebec's other major regional carrier. But by the end of the year, CP Air itself was about to be swallowed by PWA.

Ironically, CP Air's president during its final days was Donald Carty, now executive vice-president of AMR Corporation, the parent of American Airlines, and a leading figure in its decision to invest in CAIL. When he became CP Air's president in March 1985, he was only thirty-eight years old. Born in Toronto, he attended Queen's University at Kingston, Ontario and then the Harvard Graduate School of Business Administration. Subsequently, Carty worked in various financial positions at Air Canada and the Canadian Pacific Railway as well as for Celanese Canada. Then, in 1978, at the age of thirty-two, he joined American Airlines and rose meteorically through its ranks.

In 1980, his ability was recognized by the creation of a new position for him, called vice-president, profit improvement. American's profits desperately needed improving. It suffered a hefty loss of U.S.$76 million in 1980 as discount carriers attracted much of the established airlines' business through offering much lower fares in the two years following the introduction of deregulation in the United States. Carty's assignment was to restore American to profitability.

He implemented a hub-and-spoke routing and scheduling system at Chicago and Dallas, two of the busiest U.S. airports. He sold American's older planes and replaced them with newer ones that were more fuel efficient.

Some of Carty's other cost-saving measures caused discomfort for passengers and hardship for employees. Extra rows of seats were crowded into the planes. As a result, American made more money but passengers had the unpleasant experience of being squeezed into cramped space with reduced legroom. He also took severe action to decrease labour costs by eliminating 7,000 jobs, following which he introduced a two-tiered wage structure for remaining employees. In return for job security they agreed that all new employees would be hired at cut-rate wages. For example, new pilots were hired at half the previous salary level.

Having accomplished his profit-improvement task, Carty was appointed senior vice-president and controller of both American and AMR, a holding company established in 1982. But his further progress was blocked since the top positions of president and chief operating officer were both held by one person – Robert Crandall. Crandall, only eleven years Carty's senior, had earned the nickname "Fang" because of his toughness. Thus Carty was available when CP Air interviewed him, several Air Canada executives, and some non-airline ones to succeed Daniel Colussy as president.

Colussy had decided to resign in December 1984 in order to start an aviation supply business back in the United States, his home country, although he did agree to remain as CP Air's chairman and commuted back and forth. Colussy says Carty was selected because "as a very experienced airline person and as a native Canadian, he was the ideal choice." Also, since American, like CP Air, owned hotels, Carty was doubly equipped for his new job.

Thanks to Colussy's routing and marketing innovations, CP Air was profitable when Carty succeeded him in March 1985. Therefore, Carty focused on how CP Air could strengthen its presence in Eastern Canada, Air Canada's stronghold. Although CP Air had owned Eastern Provincial Airways, the leading Atlantic Canada airline since 1984, it had been shut out of local business in Ontario and Quebec for thirty years since trading its local routes in the two provinces in 1955 to Air Canada (then Trans-Canada Air Lines) in return for the Toronto-Mexico City route. The swap was part of CP Air's effort to build up an international network.

Carty believed the answer was the acquisition of Nordair, a highly successful Quebec regional airline. Nordair flew from Montreal west to the Ontario cities of Toronto, Windsor, Sudbury and Sault Ste. Marie, as well as northeast to Arctic communities.

Because of its entangled ownership, acquiring Nordair turned out to be a protracted process, taking from November 1985 until August 1986. Since 1984, Nordair had been 65 percent owned by Nordair employees and Innocan, a Montreal venture capital firm partly owned by Air Canada, and 35 percent by the Quebec government. The government had purchased its shares in 1981 when it had forestalled Nordair, then entirely owned by Air Canada, from buying Quebecair, an eastern Quebec regional airline.

The roles were reversed in September 1985 when Quebecair made a takeover bid for Nordair. Because Quebecair was losing money, money-making Nordair did not want to be bought by Quebecair and consequently sought an escape route. In November, the employees and Innocan sold their 65 percent to CP Air, but the Quebec government refused to sell its shares. Although its refusal prevented CP Air from fully absorbing Nordair into its operations, substantial integration was achieved through listing Nordair flights in its schedules and planning Nordair's flights to coincide with its own.

The struggle between Nordair and Quebecair culminated in August 1986. Nordair Metro, a commuter airline partly owned by Nordair, and therefore also by CP Air, bought Quebecair for about $10 million, outbidding by $1 million an association of Quebecair employees backed by Air Canada. Simultaneously, the Quebec government sold its 35 percent interest in Nordair to CP Air.

Thus, by the fall of 1986, CP Air was the largest it had ever been in terms of what it owned. But size did not produce a strong balance sheet. The company was already reeling from a huge loss the previous year, one of its biggest, due to an unfortunate conjunction of events. Inflation had pushed up costs, while at the same time revenue had been driven down by a fare war with Air Canada plus a strike sparked by workers' anger at concessions demanded by management following de facto deregulation under "Freedom To Move." In addition, all the acquisitions had swelled CP Air's already substantial debt to about $600 million.

Canadian Pacific, CP Air's parent, had tolerated CP Air's frequent bounce from profitability to losses for many years, both because its initial investment had been slight and because the airline's reputation for good service had offset its railway's for the reverse. CP Air's latest troubles coincided with CP's overall decision to review its portfolio. Besides CP Air, CP's broad assortment of businesses included rail and truck transportation, mining, forestry, steel and telecommunications. All are extremely capital intensive and subject to cyclical economic downturns. Therefore, CP decided to reduce its vulnerability by selling some of its interests, including CP Air.

CP's decision to sell CP Air was concurrent with PWA's desire to expand. After buying into Time Air in 1984, PWA had considered also buying Eastern Provincial and Nordair so as to gain access to the Eastern Canada market. Acquiring these airlines would have turned PWA into a national system consisting of a confederation of regional airlines. But on reflection, the company decided to drop out of the bidding and CP Air acquired the two firms. Subsequently, PWA proposed a cooperative agreement to Quebecair, but nothing came of the suggestion because PWA was hit by a strike and then Quebecair became part of Nordair Metro. Of course, when PWA later acquired CP Air, it also obtained what had been Eastern Provincial Airways, Nordair and Quebecair.

In 1985, while CP Air and Air Canada both suffered losses of more than $20 million, PWA's streak of profitability continued unbroken even though like Air Canada and CP Air it was hit by a strike over labour cost-saving measures imposed in response to the "Freedom To Move" deregulation policy. PWA's flight attendants, baggage handlers and maintenance crews struck for four months over PWA's demand for 160 work concessions. In view of PWA's profits, they believed the demands were unjustified. During the strike, union members and replacement workers were assaulted, court injunctions against picket lines were imposed, and workers alleged the security firm hired by PWA had engaged in dirty tricks. At one point, the strikers even picketed president Rhys Eyton's home.

Eyton stood fast, however, and the unions ultimately yielded. In 1986, PWA made a record profit of $39 million – three times that of 1985. Eyton believed the company was in excellent shape to expand. As in 1984, he toyed with the idea of diversification into non-airline business but, just as had happened in 1984, decided it best not to stray afield.

The decision to buy CP Air was made after Air Canada turned down his proposal of a PWA-Air Canada affiliation. Aware that Air Canada was preparing to move from government ownership to privatization, he suggested that Air Canada be the national and international flag carrier and PWA its regional network. In return, Eyton wanted PWA to receive one-third of Air Canada's stock when it privatized. That would have made PWA the single largest and thereby controlling shareholder of the much bigger Air Canada, a prospect that Air Canada loathed. Thus, it rejected Eyton's suggestion. Later, in 1992-93, when PWA rebuffed a merger with Air Canada in favour of the proposed one-third ownership by AMR Corporation, both PWA and Air Canada executives were to recollect PWA's 1986 proposal with "what if" emotions.

Having been refused by Air Canada, PWA turned its attention to CP Air, Canada's other transcontinental airline. Not long before, it had been CP Air that had broached the idea of a merger to Eyton, but he had not been interested. "We would have loved to hook up with PWA, but the discussions never got serious and a specific offer was never made," Colussy says.

Shortly afterwards, PWA became the hunter and CP Air the prey. Eyton, who had become chairman and chief executive officer of PWA in August 1986, a month before his fifty-first birthday, and thirty-eight-year-old Murray Sigler, whom Eyton had appointed his successor as president, began working on a takeover proposal in the fall. Most of the final details were drafted in front of a television set as they watched that year's exciting Grey Cup football game in which the Hamilton Tiger-Cats defeated the Edmonton Eskimos, the oddsmakers' favourite. Two days later, on December 2, PWA announced it would pay $300 million for CP Air (excluding CP Hotels), effective February 1987. It also agreed to assume CP Air's close to $600-million debt load.

The acquisition was the largest until then in Canadian aviation history. Eyton had fulfilled PWA founder Russell Baker's long-ago ambition of the 1950s that PWA became a foremost national and international airline. On the other hand, the acquisition spelled the demise of one of Canada's oldest airline names – CP Air. In 1986, CP Air was forty-four years old.

The acquisition catapulted PWA into the big leagues. In addition to swelling its number of employees from 2,700 to 13,000, and its revenue from $352 million in 1986 to $1.87 billion in 1987, the new combined company converted PWA into a global airline serving eighty-nine centres on five continents.

In April 1987, two months after the transaction was completed, PWA named the merged operations Canadian Airlines International (CAIL). "Buying CP Air was a logical fit because it increased PWA's revenue base, gave it access to world routes, and brought it one step closer to being a true competitor to Air Canada," says Peter Wallis, then a senior PWA executive.

PWA managed to afford to buy the much larger CP Air largely through making use of "hidden equity" – the planes it owned. It sold eleven and arranged a sale-leaseback of five more for a total of $255 million. PWA also issued new stock of which 75 percent of the proceeds – $275 million – was used to reduce the CP Air associated debt. The large sum PWA spent on acquiring CP Air was a marked departure for what Eyton proudly described as "a Corporation known for its strong, financially conservative management team," a description with which airline analysts agreed. Eyton pointed out potential cost savings of route coordination and bulk purchasing that the combined operations would yield.

PWA hoped CP Air's top executives, especially president Donald Carty, would remain, but in March, just a month after the takeover, he quit along with four former CP Air vice-presidents. Such resignations are common in any merger because the number of managers tends to exceed the number of top positions. As Carty said, "In the final analysis, we have fewer management positions in this organization than we have competent people." One month later, he rejoined American Airlines as senior vice-president, planning. In 1988 he became senior vice-president and chief financial officer of AMR and in 1989 executive vice-president as well as chief financial officer.

As AMR's key planning and financial executive, Carty oversees a broad range of activities: expansion of American's route system, selection of aircraft, development of new business opportunities, construction of the airline's terminals and ground facilities around the world, and cargo services. In addition, he is in charge of AMR's fast-growing contract services — transportation consulting, investment management for more than 150 major institutions including pension funds and bank and trust companies, and data processing management. AMR also develops reservations systems and undertakes ground and aircraft cabin maintenance functions for other airlines. Because of these responsibilities, Carty handled most of the negotiations with Rhys Eyton, his former employer of one month, about AMR's proposed $246 million investment in CAIL.

(Carty's younger brother, Douglas, is vice-president, finance, and treasurer of PWA and CAIL, but he did not participate in the AMR-PWA negotiations. He joined PWA in 1990; previously, he worked in corporate finance at the Bank of Nova Scotia.)

PWA's purchase of CP Air was just one of many developments in the second half of the 1980s that negated deregulation's objectives of more choice, and hence more competition in fares and service than before deregulation. Not only did Air Canada and PWA have a transcontinental duopoly, they also came to dominate the local routes feeding into them through buying or establishing the major regional carriers in each part of the country. In addition, PWA acquired Wardair, Canada's third national carrier, in 1989. Thus, by the end of the decade Canada's airline industry primarily consisted of two major airlines — Air Canada and PWA.

Air Canada's regional network consists of 100 percent-owned Air Nova (Atlantic Canada, Ottawa, Quebec City, Boston); 75 percent-owned Air Alliance (province of Quebec and Ottawa); 100 percent-owned Air Ontario (Ontario, Montreal, Winnipeg, Northeastern United States); 85 percent-owned AirBC (Western Canada, Portland, Seattle); and 100 percent-owned NWT Air (Northwest Territories, Edmonton, Winnipeg).

For its part, PWA also assembled a group of five regionals: 45 percent-owned Air Atlantic; 70 percent-owned Inter-Canadien (Quebec and Ontario); 100 percent-owned Ontario Express; 45 percent-owned Calm Air International (northern Manitoba); 100 percent-owned Time Air (Western Canada, Seattle, Minneapolis). Inter-Canadien was the product of the consolidation of Nordair Metro, Quebecair and Inter Quebec, a Quebecair subsidiary, following Nordair Metro's 1986 acquisition of Quebecair. Air Atlantic's majority owner purchased PWA's interest in late 1993, but the airline remains a CAIL connector.

Deregulation prompted the formation of these rival regional networks. "Due to deregulation, every carrier had access to every market," explains Darcy Little, general manager, Air Canada Regional Holdings. "Thus, while Air Canada was planning for international expansion, it also wanted a catchbasin in Canada to protect its domestic markets against the encroachment of start-ups." PWA felt similarly.

However, deregulation was just one reason why Air Canada and PWA established regional networks. These networks also made it possible for them to increase the number of local flights and consequently their market share, while at the same time decrease their operating costs by switching to smaller planes. Until then, both airlines had used big jets on short as well as long distances, even though there were far fewer passengers per flight. The regionals were also able to save money because they could pay lower salaries, sometimes as much as 50 percent less than the main lines. In addition, the regionals provided Air Canada and PWA with easier access to the U.S. market because under the Canada-U.S. air transport agreement, planes with fewer than sixty seats can fly cross-border, whereas larger planes must obtain government approval, a long, tedious process. Most regional planes seat fewer than sixty people.

"Before we started Air Alliance, Air Canada was flying three DC-9s, with one hundred 'economy' fare seats, between Montreal and Quebec City with a load factor of only fifty percent compared to the break-even percentage point of the mid-sixties," Little says. "Therefore, Air Canada was losing money on this route. On Air Alliance, however, we can provide twenty flights a day because we just use Dash-8-100s which seat thirty-seven passengers and have a break-even load factor in the low forties."

Besides decreasing operating costs by flying smaller planes on the route, Air Alliance has increased the choice of flight times for passengers and, consequently, its market share. "Previously, when there were only flights at 8:00 a.m., noon, and 5:30 p.m., people used alternative modes of transportation – car, bus or train – when they wanted to travel at other times," he explains. "Now, there are flights available throughout the day, so these other methods no longer have to be used. Thus, we are getting more business."

In 1992, the regionals accounted for 16 percent of the combined passenger revenue of Air Canada and PWA and 27 percent of their combined passenger traffic. Air Canada's regionals were profitable in 1992, unlike the main line; both PWA's regionals and Canadian Airlines International, its main line, were unprofitable.

To ensure that ongoing traffic flows to and from their main "trunk" line and their connectors, Air Canada and PWA prohibit their regionals from interline agreements with other carriers. This gives them a virtual monopoly over the "feeding" of regional passengers into their "trunk" line. As the 1992 Report of the Royal Commission on National Passenger Transportation concluded: "In effect, they block new entrants to trunk routes." Their domination of regional traffic also provides Air Canada and PWA with the bulk of Canada's substantial local traffic, which is far greater in proportion to that in the United States. Only 10 percent to 30 percent of regional passengers in Canada transfer to a trunk line, compared to 50 percent in the United States.

Of the regional airlines that Air Canada and PWA bought, AirBC's ownership history is the most distinctive. First, it was privately-owned. Then it sought an association with PWA. When PWA declined, AirBC formed an association with CP Air. Finally, when PWA was on the verge of buying CP Air, AirBC was sold to Air Canada, CP Air's chief rival.

AirBC was the name British Columbia entrepreneur James Pattison gave in 1980 to five small West Coast airlines he had acquired the previous year. Pattison's aim was to create a regional alternative to PWA. It was his misfortune that what seemed good timing to buy turned out to be the reverse. In the 1970s the airline business was booming and it seemed there was no end in sight to opportunities for growth. Just a few years proved Pattison had been overly optimistic. The forestry industry, the base of AirBC's business, had fallen into a slump as part of the overall economic downturn in 1982. Simultaneously, Pattison, who had acquired the airlines through leveraged buyouts, was caught in a financial squeeze when interest rates soared to record highs.

In 1983, Pattison handed over the problem to Iain Harris, an executive at the Pattison Group's headquarters. Harris was "temporarily" appointed managing director; more than ten years later he is still there, now holding the title of president. When Harris took over at the then troubled AirBC, he decided "a dramatic shift was necessary" to ensure its future. He believed that shift should be from "float" planes suitable only for coastal flights to pressurized aircraft that could handle more business because they seat more people and can be flown in the interior over the Rockies. Having also concluded that AirBC could not generate enough business on its own to justify buying the new planes, he came up with the idea of a partnership with a larger airline whereby each would feed traffic to the other.

First, he went to PWA, a logical choice since PWA was the dominant carrier in British Columbia. He pointed out that by handing over interior routes to AirBC and its smaller forty- to fifty-seat planes, PWA could redeploy the much bigger planes it was flying – often virtually empty – to busier routes. But, PWA did not want to give up this business.

Harris was left with two other options – CP Air and Air Canada. Since Air Canada was fed traffic in British Columbia by PWA and PWA affiliate Time Air, Harris was limited to a single choice – CP Air. Fortunately for him, CP Air's president Daniel Colussy liked Harris's suggestion that AirBC connect Victoria, Nanaimo and other places on Vancouver Island to CP Air's hub at Vancouver. As a result, AirBC became the first commuter carrier in Canada to formally have a commercial arrangement with a major carrier, including code-sharing.

Under code-sharing agreements, each participant lists its affiliate's or affiliates' flights as part of its own network. The advantage to a smaller airline such as AirBC is that its flights are integrated under its partner's flight designation code on travel agents' computer display screens. Consequently, they are placed higher than they otherwise would be, making them more readily seen and booked by agents.

The arrangement allowed AirBC to achieve its goal of upgrading its equipment and CP Air to save money by redeploying the big jets it was flying between Vancouver and Victoria to long-haul routes. "It had cost us a fortune to use those jets for such a short distance," Colussy recollects. The cooperative agreement began in October 1983 and, by 1985, AirBC had become one of Canada's most successful commuter airlines, carrying 550,000 passengers. It exchanged 6,000 passengers a month with CP Air, which had synchronized its schedule with AirBC's and arranged for AirBC planes to load and unload at CP Air's Vancouver airport section.

In that each benefited, both sides expected their arrangement to last a long time. But in November 1986, just three years after it had begun, AirBC began to hear rumours that PWA might buy CP Air and merge their operations. Harris was concerned that a merger could render AirBC "potentially redundant because PWA owned 44 percent of Time Air and would naturally favour the continuation of that relationship" to one with AirBC.

To make certain that AirBC would not wind up a loser, Harris telephoned Air Canada's head office in Montreal to ascertain whether it would be interested in buying AirBC. He pointed out: "Air Canada has a lot to lose, too, if such a merger occurs because it has no presence in British Columbia beyond Vancouver and Victoria." By contrast, he went on, PWA, CP Air and Time Air were all well represented. Air Canada accepted his reasoning and agreed to buy 85 percent of AirBC. Harris owns the rest. Air Canada made its offer the last week of November and one week later PWA announced its intention of buying CP Air.

Considering that AirBC and CP Air had been mutually satisfied with their arrangement, AirBC's decision to join the competition evoked strong reaction at CP Air. Colussy says he was "amazed." Harris recalls that "people at CP Air were mad at us for a few days because they felt we had abrogated our relationship with their camp, but they came to realize that we had done what was best for AirBC." Coincidentally, PWA's takeover of CP Air and Air Canada's of AirBC were both finalized in February 1987.

Air Canada and Harris each give a different version as to why Harris owns 15 percent. Air Canada Regional Holdings' general manager Darcy Little points out that since Air Canada was still a Crown corporation at the time, any 100 percent-owned subsidiary would have also been subject to the federal government's jurisdiction. Harris, however, says he was given the 15 percent share as an inducement for him to stay on as AirBC's president.

While Air Canada and PWA were busily building up their regional networks in anticipation of formal deregulation, the "Freedom To Move" policy paper became the basis of the "National Transportation Act, 1987." The Act came into effect as of January 1, 1988. It stipulated that market forces, rather than economic regulation, should govern the supply of air services and replaced the twenty-year-old Canadian Transport Commission with the National Transportation Agency.

The Agency's duties include resolving disputes between carriers and shippers or travellers over rates and services as well as licensing Canadian and foreign carriers operating in Canada and Canadian airlines operating abroad. Because the National Transportation Act requires 75 percent of the voting interest of Canadian airlines to be Canadian-owned, the Agency held hearings in March 1993 on AMR's proposed $246 million investment in Canadian Airlines International in return for a 25 percent voting and one-third percent equity interest. Besides dealing with various airline matters, the Agency issues rail certificates, manages rail subsidy programs, and evaluates proposals for decreasing rail service.

* * *

The many changes in the 1980s often triggered still more. But it was deregulation that was the prime catalyst of the events in the second half of the decade, starting with the national duopoly of Air Canada and PWA assembling regional duopolies and proceeding to Air Canada's privatization and PWA's purchase of Wardair.

Privatization had been the goal of Air Canada's Claude Taylor since the late 1970s. He had discussed partial privatization with Transport Minister Otto Lang when Lang ended Air Canada's status as a Canadian National Railways subsidiary and converted it into a separate Crown corporation under the 1977 Air Canada Act. However, both men regarded Air Canada as being unprivatizable because of its weak balance sheet. Air Canada had

had combined losses of $32 million between 1974 and 1976, and its working capital had dropped from $98.6 million in 1975 to $14.7 million in 1976.

Hence, investing in Air Canada at that time would have had no appeal to stock market investors. Ironically, as it turned out the company's 1974 to 1976 losses were only a minute fraction of the $746 million lost between 1990 and 1992 following privatization in 1988-89; as a result, unfortunate shareholders earned absolutely nothing per share. Aside from financial drawbacks, privatization did not proceed in the late 1970s because of politics – a fellow Cabinet minister successfully opposed Lang, maintaining that even partial privatization would too greatly weaken the government's authority over such a prominent Crown corporation.

Although privatization was shelved in 1977, Claude Taylor did not drop the idea. In his view, Air Canada was at a disadvantage because, unlike private airlines, its financing plans, capital budgets and acquisitions had to gain three-way approval from the Treasury Board, the Department of Finance and the Department of Transport. The government's control over its finances placed Air Canada in a dilemma as the 1980s progressed because it urgently needed to buy new planes so as to remain competitive against domestic and international carriers that were modernizing their fleets.

Much of Air Canada's fleet needed replacing due to age and above-average fuel consumption and maintenance costs. While the airline did acquire twelve new planes in 1983, which it had ordered in 1979, they accounted for only 10 percent of its total aircraft and were far below the industry replacement rate of ten new planes a year.

Air Canada estimated it needed forty-three new planes. Because the total cost would come to a staggering $3 billion, equivalent to the value at that time of its entire assets, the company decided to limit its purchase to half and lease the rest. Even so, it still required a lot of money. Since its retained earnings were insufficient and it did not want to increase its debt load, it decided it needed new equity to apply to the purchases. There were two ways it could obtain the equity – from its present owner, the federal government, or through a public share offering, provided the government would be willing to privatize it.

The first option had no chance because the government had no intention of bankrolling the fleet purchase. At that time, the government's equity in Air Canada was slightly more than $300 million. Thus, to have allocated that money entirely for new planes would have been irresponsible. The government's deficit was high and there were huge demands on its resources from many directions, including Air Canada's arch rival, fellow Crown corporation Via Rail. Therefore, the Trudeau government and subsequently the Mulroney government refused to infuse fresh capital into Air Canada.

At the same time, Trudeau and then Mulroney were reluctant to allow Air Canada to privatize in order to increase its funds from a public share issue. When Mulroney was asked shortly after his election as prime minister in 1984 whether Air Canada would be privatized, he adamantly declared that it was "not for sale." But he was contradicted by his transport minister, Donald Mazankowski, who said, "We are going to give Air Canada and Canadian National Railways the freedom to run their affairs like a private company in anticipation of profit." Mazankowski's comment was given more weight than Mulroney's because, as former transport minister, Liberal Lloyd Axworthy, pointed out: "Can one realistically say it is possible to have a competitive environment when Air Canada still has a financial umbilical cord tied to the Cabinet? Is this really fair competition?"

Also, the Conservatives thought that privatization of Air Canada would score them points with Canadian voters who shared the mood growing worldwide in free-enterprise countries that governments had become too deeply involved in the economy. Certainly, it was Claude Taylor's belief that despite Mulroney's assertion to the contrary, Air Canada would be sold by the government. "Although I had been agitating for privatization for many years, it was not until 1984-85 that it seemed likely to become a reality," he recollects.

Convinced that the government's attitude had changed, he wrote in Air Canada's 1985 annual report that the airline was "determined to manage its own destiny, to compete actively and on an equal basis with all airlines, and to achieve a standard of financial credibility that will ultimately enable the shareholder [the government] to pursue a course of private and employee equity participation."

The pledge of "financial credibility" referred to the fact that to be privatizable, Air Canada needed to improve its profitability and substantially lower its debt-to-equity ratio. The ratio was 69 percent in 1983; it was cut to 27 percent by 1989, the year privatization was completed.

The reduction was accomplished in many ways. Perpetual loans of over $800 million, amounting to quasi-equity, were obtained on the Swiss and Japanese financial markets. Thirty-five older planes were sold to Federal Express as part of the modernization plan whereby new planes would replace old ones. Demand for older planes was then strong, and the FedEx deal was negotiated at a higher price than is obtainable today.

Labour costs were markedly decreased by means of a wage freeze combined with longer working hours, as well as the elimination of four hundred management positions. Advance timetable planning was shortened from twelve to just two months, ending the costly slack time of previous long-range forecasts. Also, a regional cross-country network of affiliated airlines feeding traffic into the main line was developed.

The outcome of all these measures was that Air Canada's balance sheet became sufficiently healthy by 1988 for the government, despite Mulroney's "not for sale" pledge, to begin privatizing the airline. Thus, on April 12, 1988, the government announced that 45 percent would initially be sold to the public. It decided to sell the company in two phases, both because there were doubts as to whether the marketplace could absorb a single large offering and because it was hoped that if the company did well after the first issue, the second could be sold at a higher price.

The timing of the announcement was significant. It was made the same day Air Canada reported a 1987 profit of $45.7 million – $5.3 million more than in 1986, notwithstanding a strike that had shut it down for nineteen days. Additionally, the announcement came less than two weeks after Mazankowski's appointment as the minister responsible for the government's privatization efforts. Mazankowski had become deputy prime minister in 1986 after two years as minister of transport.

Preparations for the 45 percent offering took several months, and the sale did not start until mid-September. Some Canadians wondered why they should buy shares in something they already owned, but thousands who rarely or never invested in the stock market flooded stockbrokers' offices with requests for information. For its part, Air Canada took the usual course of advertising the share issue in newspapers in stark contrast to the flamboyant 1986 privatization promotion of British Airways (formerly British Overseas Airways Corporation) which included a sound-and-light show with fireworks and a flypast by its Concorde airplane.

Through its company newspaper and notices in its computerized reservations system, Air Canada encouraged its then 23,000 employees to invest, too. More than 17,000 did, making them one of the largest employee-investor groups in Canada.

In this initial offering, Air Canada's shares were sold at $8 each. But despite the public's curiosity, supply turned out to exceed demand and only 43 percent of the 45 percent available shares were sold. The shares quickly fell below the initial price, but in January 1989 they received a boost from an unexpected source when PWA announced it would take over Wardair. That announcement suddenly made Air Canada's shares attractive to investors in anticipation of the reduction in the number of carriers from three to two, easing the deep discounting of fares and thereby increasing profits.

By April 1989, Air Canada's shares had risen to $12 – 50 percent more than their issue value. Therefore, although the government had protected itself against a possible price drop by saying it might take as long as ten years to make the second share offering, it was able to proceed shortly after the minimum one-year waiting period expired on April 13, 1989. It set May 17 as the date for the announcement.

It got a scare when the price dropped slightly below $12 just two days before in response to Air Canada's reporting a loss for its first quarter, always a slow travel period and consequently a low revenue earner compared to the peak summer months. However, by the next day the price recovered and the government went ahead on schedule. The sale was completed in July. The proceeds from the two-stage sale came to $707.8 million. This cash infusion enabled Air Canada to go ahead with its orders for forty-three planes.

The long time it took to privatize Air Canada, both because of its financial weakness and the government's reluctance to sell it, can be partly blamed for Air Canada's overcapacity problems today. Had it been able to order its new planes in the mid-1980s, it would have received them when the market for older planes was still strong and they could be easily sold. But the delay resulted in its new planes being delivered primarily after 1990 when the demand for old planes had evaporated due to the recession.

For Air Canada's shareholders, the stock has been mostly a disappointment. The highest price it reached was $14.88 and that was back in 1989. In 1992 and 1993, the value sank as low as $2.20.

During its fifty-one years of government ownership, Air Canada amply fulfilled its mandate to be a national carrier and thereby be a factor in Canada's economic development. In the years immediately prior to its privatization, it failed only twice to make a profit and that was in 1982 and 1985 when the economic downturns adversely affected every industry. In 1988, at the start of its privatization, its profit of $99 million was more than double that of 1987; and in 1989, on the completion of its privatization, its profit spiralled to $149 million. Its long investment in Air Canada paid off well for the federal government. Between 1938 and 1987, various Liberal and Conservative governments gave Air Canada $750 million in equity investments, loans and advances; in return, Air Canada paid back $1 billion in principal, interest and dividends.

* * *

April 1989 was also a turning point for Canada's two other major carriers – PWA and Wardair. On April 24, PWA acquired Wardair for $250.8 million.

Throughout its thirty-six years, Wardair was headed by its founder, Max Ward. A hard-driving entrepreneur, he built Wardair into Canada's third-largest airline as well as its leading charter carrier with an outstanding worldwide reputation. But the very expansion that had made it so big had also weakened it financially, making it vulnerable to a takeover.

Maxwell William (Max) Ward was born in Edmonton in 1921. In 1940, he joined the Royal Canadian Air Force, received his pilot's wings, and served as a commissioned flight instructor at various Canadian bases until 1945. When World War II ended, he worked as a bush pilot for a year, flying from northern Alberta to the Northwest Territories. Then, in 1946, he started his own company, Polaris Charter, with a single-engine plane for which he paid $12,500, about three times his financial worth. Based in Yellowknife, Polaris Charter flew supplies and passengers to the booming mining industry in the vicinity. As was the fate with many undercapitalized bush operations, Polaris did not last long. It failed after just one year. Ward then worked for other bush companies and also briefly went into home construction in Lethbridge, Alberta.

But by 1953 he was back in the aviation business with the formation of Wardair, based at Yellowknife, as Polaris Charter had been. Again, he started with only one plane. He bought more as business grew, including some freight planes that Trans-Canada Air Lines (now Air Canada) decided to sell in 1957. These planes enabled Ward to pioneer the air transport of heavy equipment into the far Arctic; on one occasion the landing point was the North Pole, the northernmost point of the earth's axis.

In 1962, Ward began flying four-engined freighter aircraft to high-latitude operations, carrying fourteen-ton loads of construction equipment into semi-prepared landing strips. That same year he acquired a licence from the federal government's Air Transport Board to begin international commercial flights, and in June inaugurated a passenger charter business with an Edmonton-to-Copenhagen route. It was the first overseas charter flight operation serving Western Canada.

International charter flights have become so commonplace that most Canadians today probably do not comprehend the magnitude of the risk Ward undertook. In 1962, charter flights were in their infancy and few foresaw that they would become extraordinarily popular. Ward was one of the few and got his headstart by taking advantage of a loophole in the rules governing international flights. World War II bombing had been so devastating that the victorious Allies wanted to make certain that their air space would be safe in peacetime. Therefore, they established the International Civil Aviation Organization (ICAO), headquartered in Montreal, to coordinate international civil aviation, including standard safety measures and the negotiation of scheduled flights between countries.

However, the ICAO established very few rules concerning non-scheduled charter flights. Because few individuals could afford to charter an airline for an international flight, the scheduled airlines were confident that charters would never be a threat to them. But to make absolutely certain, the ICAO stipulated that groups which did arrange charter flights must be genuine and not organized for the sole purpose of chartering an aircraft.

What the scheduled airlines neglected to take into consideration was the ingenuity of the charter operators and the enthusiasm of bargain-seeking travellers who were overjoyed at the prospect of cheap charter fares. The charters could afford to charge far less because their operating expenses were much lower and they tended to be fully booked. Because charters treated all passengers equally with only one seat size and one meal choice, their operators did not have the expenses that the scheduled airlines' economy, business and first classes require in a variety of seat configurations and meals. Moreover, whereas the charter airlines flew only in peak travelling periods, the scheduled airlines flew year-round. Therefore, they charged more to compensate for their load factor averaging only 60 percent due to seasonal irregularity of traffic flow.

It was not long until the ICAO rules were circumvented by the formation of "affinity clubs," many of whose members had more affinity with the clubs' charter flights than with their stated purpose. In some cases, ski clubs that went on charter flights included frail, eighty-year-old grandmothers; in others, overnight memberships were backdated six months!

Countries whose scheduled airlines belonged to the ICAO were torn between welcoming the tourist revenue of charter flights or discouraging them to protect their scheduled airlines. Unsurprisingly, the lure of tourist revenue won out. Consequently, international charter airlines like Wardair flourished. By 1973, after just nine years in the business, Wardair was flying all over the world to England, Europe, the Mediterranean countries, the Caribbean, the United States, the Far East and the South Pacific islands.

It earned a stellar reputation and affection among travellers for treating them like first-class passengers rather than cheap bargain hunters. Wardair flights provided free bar service, steak served on Royal Doulton porcelain with linen-covered trays and stainless steel cutlery, at fares well below standard economy-class levels. Canadians reacted by flocking away from the more expensive Air Canada and CP Air flights.

It was an impressive achievement. But it had also severely strained Wardair's finances because it had necessitated buying many new planes, and at that time one jumbo jet alone cost $25 million. Thus, Wardair's appearance of success concealed the reality of distress, and Ward looked for a buyer to come to the rescue. Some years earlier, he had tried to sell Wardair to CP Air, but although CP Air's then-president Jack Gilmore was enthused, Ian Sinclair, then chairman of Canadian Pacific, CP Air's parent, was not.

In 1973, Ward decided to approach CP Air's rival, Air Canada. He offered Air Canada one-third of Wardair's shares outright for $2.7 million, with an option to purchase another third and proposed that Wardair in effect became Air Canada's charter division. The suggested price was equal to about 10 percent of the prevailing cost of a jumbo jet and to just slightly more than 1 percent of what PWA paid to acquire all of Wardair sixteen years later in 1989.

However, the proposal died a quick death. The Consumers' Association of Canada objected, arguing that travellers would suffer because the deal would lessen competition. Air Canada's pilots were also opposed, fearing Air Canada would transfer the jumbo jets it had on order to Wardair thereby affecting either their pay or their jobs; Wardair paid less than Air Canada.

Also, a change in Canadian government rules covering charters gave scheduled carriers like Air Canada a small wedge into the charter market. As a result, there was no need for Air Canada to acquire Wardair as its charter arm. In 1972, scheduled airlines had been allowed to start offering "advance-booking charters," eroding the distinction between them and charter operators because blocks of seats could now be sold without the requirement that the individual purchasers have any affiliation with one another. In 1976, Air Canada introduced "charter-class" fares on its regularly scheduled flights between Canada and the United Kingdom. The new fares made it cheaper to fly across the Atlantic than across Canada, and soon Canadians began demanding equal treatment at home.

Air Canada and CP Air responded the next year by introducing domestic "charter-class" fares but there were so many restrictions, known as "fences," that few benefited. Trips had to cover more than seven hundred miles, be booked sixty days in advance, and passengers had to stay at least ten days at their destination. Even if travellers could meet all these criteria, there were few charter-class seats available per flight.

The scheduled airlines' overseas charter fares were a direct blow aimed at Wardair. What made the situation more frustrating was the federal government's refusal to allow Wardair to offer charter services in Canada. "We were in a ball game where the umpire owned the bat and ball – and the house team," Max Ward later complained in his memoirs published two years after he sold Wardair. "Not many calls went the way of the Visitors, and we were always the Visitors." For years, Ward protested in vain that it was unfair on the part of the federal government to let the scheduled carriers invade his turf, yet prevent him from encroaching on theirs.

Finally, in 1980, Wardair was permitted to start offering charter service between major Canadian cities, thus placing it in direct competition with

Canada's leading national and regional airlines. Shortly afterward, the entire industry was buffeted by the overall economic recession. Wardair was so badly off that it faced bankruptcy, and Ward's meetings with his bankers were a challenge to his survival skills – a challenge that he adroitly met. There was the time, for example, when in order to avoid answering unpleasant probing questions, he referred them to two associates; as one was hard of hearing and the other stuttered badly when under intense pressure, that meeting fizzled!

Ward saved Wardair by that old standby of airlines when in trouble – he sold some planes. He also continued to press the federal government to extend scheduled rights to Wardair so that it could compete on a fully equal basis with Air Canada and CP Air and subsequently Canadian Airlines International after CP Air was acquired by PWA in 1987 and its operations merged with PWA's. In 1985, the government licensed Wardair to operate scheduled international service and, in 1986, domestic scheduled flights. Those years were also significant to Wardair because it won some important awards. In 1985, *Holiday Which?*, a British consumer magazine, named Wardair the world's finest charter airline, based on a survey of United Kingdom travel agents. Next, the magazine selected Wardair as the world's best scheduled carrier for two years in a row – the only years, as it turned out, that Wardair was in the competition.

Wardair no longer was the "visiting" team. But just as CP Air suffered when it achieved parity with Air Canada, so did Wardair when it obtained equality with Air Canada, CP Air, and CAIL, CP Air's successor. Both CP Air and Wardair were confronted by the same difficulty – because their fleets were smaller than Air Canada's, they had to spend vast amounts of money on expansion to reach a size that would enable them to compete fully. Wardair had ten planes; to compete as a scheduled carrier, it required at least thirty. In 1987 and 1988, it ordered twelve planes at a cost of $1 billion, with the intention of obtaining ten more in 1989.

Wardair also faced other problems. It was hard for it to woo travellers away from its rivals because they ensured customer loyalty through frequent-flier programs in which travel points are built up for free trips. Wardair's counter-strategy of its own frequent-flier program as well as champagne and smoked salmon cut into its financial resources at the very time it was investing so heavily in new planes. Another difficulty was its inability to obtain well-located check-in space and gates at airports since all the good spots were held by airlines that had been there far longer.

As a result, although at its peak Wardair obtained 11 percent of the passenger kilometres flown on scheduled flights, its share of the total number of passengers was only 4.8 percent according to Statistics Canada. Moreover, that proportion had been achieved at a heavy financial toll. With only $130 million in cash, it had ten aircraft scheduled for delivery in 1989 in addition to the $1 billion worth of planes it had recently bought. In 1988, Wardair was confronted with a $21.6-million loss compared to a 1987 profit of $31 million. The prospects for 1989 were also stark – financial default if earnings did not improve. Ward anticipated a loss of around $50 million; in actuality, it was $54 million.

Today, Ward says that although Wardair was in a weak financial state, in his opinion it "was not finished by any means. Through all the years of building Wardair, I had been in difficult situations before and had got out of them; I would have got out of this one, too." But when pressed as to how, Ward merely replies that he could have obtained "money from a Canadian investor," whom he refuses to identify. He did not accept because it would have meant relinquishing control. This would have been difficult for the autocratic Ward who had run Wardair the way he saw fit throughout its entire history and was proud of expanding the airline from just one plane into Canada's third-largest carrier.

Furthermore, Ward was worried about the industry's outlook in view of the onset of the recession at a time when there was substantial fleet overcapacity in the Canadian marketplace. "The amount of overcapacity frightened me because with three airlines sharing the market, they were all going to suffer," he says. Wardair was particularly vulnerable in view of its shaky finances.

There was also the factor that Ward was sixty-eight years old, past the usual retirement age, and had been in the airline business for forty-three years. For all these reasons, he decided it would be better to sell the whole of Wardair rather than just part.

Hence, in late 1988 he asked PWA's chairman, Rhys Eyton, if PWA would be interested in buying Wardair, even though Ward believed Wardair's problems were partly due to PWA-owned Canadian Airlines International. He had been angered by CAIL's refusal to sign an interline agreement with Wardair whereby each would handle the other's baggage on connecting flights and by CAIL's insistence that separate tickets be issued for the Wardair and Canadian portions of such flights. However, single tickets often were issued by travel agents because the international system for handling flight coupons (called The Bank Settlement Plan) takes into account that passengers often have to use different carriers to reach their destination.

Although well aware of Wardair's difficulties, Eyton was attracted for a number of reasons. Buying Wardair would remove it as a competitor. Also, PWA would obtain Wardair's $1-billion worth of new planes, the youngest fleet in Canada's airline industry. Furthermore, through buying Wardair, PWA would be able for the first time to compete against Air Canada for the lucrative traffic to and from the United Kingdom and France. The Canadian government had awarded Wardair second-carrier status to both countries in 1984, but CP Air, which PWA had acquired partly for its international routes, had been shut out of both markets. That Wardair made $50 million a year from flying the United Kingdom and France routes seemed another good reason to PWA for acquiring Wardair.

The wisdom of this reasoning was quickly apparent. The Wardair purchase increased CAIL's international traffic by close to 40 percent. Consequently, half of CAIL's revenue was derived from international routes compared to 40 percent at Air Canada. Additionally, Wardair had a better image for customer service than CAIL and stronger loyalty among leisure travellers.

"We knew how badly off Wardair was, but buying it made sense," says Peter Wallis at CAIL. "Wardair had good assets in aircraft and expanded our European route network. Also, we acquired a team of service-oriented people who improved CAIL's service. Thus, although critics viewed the purchase as a lead weight around CAIL's neck, it wasn't. We recouped our investment through sales of some Wardair planes and through increased business to Europe."

Adds Murray Sigler, who was president and chief operating officer of CAIL at the time: "In hindsight, perhaps a case can be made that we should have paid less. But the strengths of Canadian Airlines today — its image of providing quality and the will of its employees to save it — are largely due to the Wardair acquisition."

While airline industry analysts concur that CAIL gained these benefits from Wardair's acquisition, they believe that Wardair's sickly state did not warrant the overly generous price PWA paid. Even though Wardair's stock had traded no higher than $16 3/8 and was as low as $7 in the months preceding, PWA paid the equivalent of $17.25 a share, the same as that at which the shares had been issued in September 1987. Ward insisted on this because he wanted the shareholders "to get their money back." Of course, as the principal shareholder, he was the chief beneficiary.

Peter Wallis says PWA acquiesced because "Max Ward and Rhys Eyton had struck a deal and PWA carried through with its obligations." But Frederick (Ted) Larkin, airline analyst at investment dealer Bunting Warburg, says it is a "mystery why PWA paid so much. Wardair was in its last throes; therefore, PWA should have walked away. Instead, it issued new shares to Ward as part of the terms of the acquisition, thereby diluting the value of PWA shares, and also absorbed Wardair's debt." The $250.8 million

PWA paid for Wardair was a mixture of cash and shares. Wardair's debt was $700 million.

Considering that Wardair was on the brink of default, Jacques Kavafian, airline analyst at investment dealer Lévesque Beaubien Geoffrion, calls the acquisition "a major mistake." Larkin describes it as an "act of desperation to remove a key competitor."

In a report written just before the acquisition was finalized, Tony Hine, airline analyst at investment dealer ScotiaMcLeod, predicted the takeover would cause problems in nearly all areas of running an airline: aircraft, pilot training and financial operating targets. "Although most of Wardair's planes were similar to those in Canadian's fleet in their size, range and mission, they lacked maintenance commonality," he explained. He also pointed out that there would be the expense of training pilots from each company to fly types of planes they had not previously flown.

As for Canadian's financial objectives, Hine noted that the acquisition of Wardair did not "meet Canadian's target of long-run operating margins of 9 percent. Wardair had annual revenue of $700 million, but it also had an equal amount of debt. It did generate $63 million in operating income, but the acquisition incurred interest expense of $90 million at an average interest cost of 10 percent."

Despite these drawbacks, PWA persisted with its takeover offer. It was briefly opposed by only AMR Corporation. In the airline industry, today's ally often was yesterday's foe. That is the case with PWA and AMR Corporation. Whereas today AMR and PWA are forging an alliance whereby AMR will help save PWA through a $246-million investment in Canadian Airlines, in 1989 AMR was PWA's opponent when it made a counter-offer for Wardair along with three Canadian partners. The Canadian partners were Penfund Management, a Toronto-based pension fund; Shieldings Inc., a Toronto-based privately-held merchant bank; and Atlantic Corporation, a St. John's, Newfoundland investment company. At that time Atlantic and Shieldings controlled Air Nova, a regional airline in Atlantic Canada that was (and is) part of the Air Canada connector network. The Canadians were involved because Canadian regulations prohibit more than 25 percent foreign ownership of a Canadian carrier.

But the bid collapsed with each side giving different explanations. The bidders said Wardair's "numbers are in such a complex form that to unravel them would take more time than we have available" to meet a deadline for counter-offers imposed by the federal Bureau of Competition Policy. Ward, however, maintained that "American had no intention whatsoever of buying into our company" and he also said that "speculation that it might step in was complete nonsense."

As no more offers were made, PWA wound up as Wardair's owner. Rhys Eyton promised to retain the Wardair name and operate it separately from Canadian Airlines International, but such a pledge was poor economics and therefore lasted for only eight and a half months. On January 1, 1990, Wardair's name disappeared when the company was amalgamated with Canadian Airlines International. Subsequently, duplication in jobs was eliminated in order to reduce expenses. CAIL laid off 1,900 workers of whom 1,017 were former Wardair employees – close to one-fifth of what Wardair's workforce had been.

* * *

The acquisition brought PWA's rising young star, Kevin Jenkins, to the forefront when he was appointed president and chief operating officer of Wardair immediately upon the takeover's completion. On being asked about how he feels Jenkins handled the position, Max Ward was somewhat brusque. His immediate response was "I wasn't there." But upon being reminded that he was there since he was on PWA's board of directors from 1989 through part of 1992, he responded: "Because one is on a board doesn't mean you know how a company is running internally, especially at a time of a takeover when things aren't normal." After a pause, Ward added: "Kevin Jenkins is a bright young fellow and competent."

Of course, Ward's reaction is understandable considering that a young man less than half his age took over the presidency of a company Ward had run for thirty-six years. Coincidentally, Jenkins was the same age – thirty-two – Ward had been when he started Wardair. Jenkins did impress PWA's chairman, Rhys Eyton, because just six months later, in October 1989, Eyton named him executive vice-president and chief operating officer of Canadian Airlines International in advance of the January 1990 amalgamation of Wardair and CAIL. Eyton doubled as president and chief executive officer of PWA and as chairman, president and chief executive officer of CAIL.

In many ways Jenkins is a twenty-two-years-younger version of Eyton, and his swift ascent largely mirrored Eyton's. Both started at PWA in the finance department and both were young when they arrived at the top. Eyton was forty-one when he became president of PWA in 1976. Jenkins was even younger – thirty-two – when he became president of Wardair in 1989 and then CAIL's executive vice-president. He was only thirty-five when he moved upwards to the presidency of CAIL in 1991.

The tall, personable Jenkins is described by analysts as "affable," but he is also known for stringent cost-cutting, including many layoffs. Born in Edmonton, he received a law degree from the University of Alberta and an

MBA from Harvard University. While there, he met Murray Sigler who was attending Harvard's advanced management program for business executives as part of his climb at PWA. The two men would later come to be regarded as competitors, although Sigler emphasizes that their ambitions lay in different directions. However, when they first met, the possibility of rivalry did not occur to either.

Sigler, nine years Jenkins's senior, contacted Jenkins at the suggestion of Jenkins's father-in-law, Egerton (Ed) King. King was chief executive officer of Canadian Utilities Limited, a large Edmonton-based gas and electricity company and a member of CAIL's board. He thought it might be nice while they were away at Harvard for both Sigler and Jenkins to meet somebody from home.

Jenkins was then considering working as a financial consultant in the United States after graduating. As Sigler recalls their conversation, he suggested that Jenkins also consider the alternative of a career at PWA because PWA's senior vice-president of finance would soon be retiring and therefore PWA would need "more bench strength." Sigler stresses that King never attempted to get his son-in-law hired by PWA and that he was "totally surprised" when Jenkins did decide to work there.

In any event, after graduating Jenkins did not immediately go to PWA. His first post-university position was as a partner in an Edmonton law firm where he specialized in corporate law. In 1986, he joined PWA's finance department and the following year he became senior financial officer, the position Sigler had told him would become open.

Jenkins and Sigler were promoted steadily at PWA. Like Jenkins, Sigler was a lawyer by training. Born in Calgary, he moved to Yellowknife after graduating from the University of Alberta in 1970. He eventually became the managing partner in the Northwest Territories' largest law firm and also served as city solicitor for a year in Yellowknife. He met Eyton by chance in a Yellowknife bar, and Eyton retained him to do some legal work for PWA.

In the late 1970s, Sigler decided he wanted to return to Calgary. PWA's headquarters had been moved there from Vancouver in 1976 by its owner of two years, the Alberta government. The transfer had prompted the resignation of Don Watson, PWA's then-president, who considered the move an unnecessary expense, and Watson had been succeeded by Eyton. In 1977, Eyton hired the thirteen-year-younger Sigler to establish an in-house legal department at PWA.

Subsequently, Sigler moved rapidly up the ranks. Within a year, he was named corporate counsel. In 1979, he became vice-president, legal and regulatory affairs; in 1982, senior vice-president, commercial services; in

1985, executive vice-president and chief operating officer of PWA; and in 1986, president. After PWA acquired CP Air and merged the two companies under the Canadian Airlines International name, Sigler became CAIL's initial president and chief operating officer. In 1989, he became executive vice-president of PWA Corporation, the parent company of all PWA's activities – CAIL, the regional airlines, and holiday tour operations – and played a major role in Wardair's acquisition that year.

Sigler maintains that he and Jenkins were not competitors because he was more interested in corporate development and Jenkins in operations. He describes his relationship with Jenkins as "friendly," but he is much closer with Eyton with whom he goes fishing. Even so, Eyton made Jenkins president of the much larger CAIL in 1991, whereas Sigler was named president of the newly formed Canadian Regional Airlines, the umbrella company for PWA's connector airlines. Sigler says that appointment fitted in with his interest in corporate development. In 1993, in advance of the realignment of Canadian Regional from a separate organization to a subsidiary of CAIL, Sigler left PWA to form his own consultancy firm, although he remained on its board of directors and restructuring committee.

In addition to affecting Sigler's and Jenkins's careers and eliminating 1,900 jobs, PWA's acquisition of Wardair had major repercussions for Canada's airline industry. The takeover resulted in what airline analysts described as "pricing stability" – an end to the fare wars and a subsequent ticket price increase, good news for the airlines' balance sheets but bad news for consumers. Air Canada and Canadian announced increases of 6 percent in March 1989, followed by a 15-percent hike in April.

The takeover also restored transcontinental airline service in Canada to a duopoly. As ScotiaMcLeod's Tony Hine commented following the acquisition: "In establishing its scheduled status, Wardair clearly disrupted Canada's status quo. Following Ward's decision to withdraw before being eliminated in the marketplace, it is fair to conclude that Canada's market can only support two national carriers."

Industry statistics underscore how Air Canada and CAIL benefited from the removal of Wardair as a competitor. In 1988, Wardair accounted for 11 percent of passenger kilometres flown and Air Canada and CAIL for 87.2 percent. In 1990, the year after CAIL absorbed Wardair, Air Canada's and CAIL's combined share jumped to 97.5 percent and has remained at or just above that level ever since. PWA's acquisition of CP Air in 1987 and of Wardair in 1989 helped boost its revenue from millions to billions of dollars. In 1986 its revenue was $352 million; in 1989, $2.7 billion. Without any acquisitions of a similar magnitude, in this same period Air

Canada's revenue climbed from $2.9 billion to $3.7 billion, a much smaller rate of growth but enough to maintain its paramountcy.

Thus, Air Canada and PWA, seemingly snug and secure as Canada's only two national airlines, had high hopes for the 1990s. But instead, the story turned out to be vastly different.

CHAPTER FIVE

Troubled Skies (1990 – 1994, Part I)

F rom 1990 through 1992, Air Canada and PWA lost more money than they had made in their entire histories. In 1992, they both suffered record losses; PWA lost $543 million and Air Canada, $454 million. On average, PWA lost $1.5 million a day, and Air Canada $1.2 million. "Air Canada and PWA could be compared to two people jumping from an office tower – PWA from the fifteenth floor and Air Canada from the thirtieth, thumbing its nose because PWA would hit the ground first," says Ted Larkin, airline industry analyst at investment dealer Bunting Warburg.

Considering their huge losses, massive multi-billion dollar debt, exhaustion of their shareholders' equity and dwindling supply of cash, both airlines were in dire distress in 1993. Nevertheless, they continued in business because their creditors figured they had more to lose by liquidating them. Since the resale market for planes was virtually dead, as a result of the worldwide decline in the airline industry, Air Canada's and PWA's creditors would not have been able to recoup much money. In taking no action the creditors were banking on optimistic predictions that the industry would revive in 1994 and strengthen further in 1995.

Although both airlines were in deep trouble from 1990 on, Air Canada was in a somewhat stronger position – on Larkin's metaphorical thirtieth floor – because it had substantially more cash and the bulk of its debt was not due until 1996. PWA was much worse off – on Larkin's metaphorical fifteenth floor – because it expected to run out of cash by the end of 1993 and needed to restructure itself financially in order to stay alive. However, at the end of 1993, PWA said it had enough cash until June 30, 1994 when it hoped the CAIL-AMR deal would become a reality.

Their struggle to survive embroiled many besides themselves in a long, complex and often ugly battle. Between 1991 and the summer of 1993, Air Canada presented three proposals for a full or partial merger to PWA, as well as an offer to buy PWA's international routes. PWA rejected the first two merger offers, made in the fall of 1991 and the summer of 1992. A pre-merger arrangement was reached on the third proposal on October 8, but Air Canada terminated it on November 3, saying it would not produce a "viable" airline. Nine months later, on August 18, 1993, it offered to buy PWA's lucrative international routes. PWA angrily refused to sell them, with chairman Rhys Eyton saying, "The whole exercise is part of a diabolical plot to kill this airline."

AMR Corporation, American Airlines' parent, twice offered to invest in PWA-owned Canadian Airlines International; its offer was accepted the second time with the deal signed December 29, 1992, subject to the approval of the Canadian government. Thus, two computerized airline reservations systems became embattled – Gemini and Sabre. Air Canada and PWA had formed Gemini in 1987. AMR stipulated that in return for its investment in Canadian Airlines International, CAIL must switch to its Sabre system.

In addition, three governments were involved – the federal and those of Alberta and British Columbia, the provinces where the bulk of PWA's employees are located. In November 1992, the federal government provided $50 million to PWA in emergency interim financing, far less than the $190 million PWA had sought. The next month, Alberta agreed to give $50 million and British Columbia $20 million in loan guarantees.

Two federal government agencies took part, too. The National Transportation Agency approved AMR's investment in Canadian Airlines International in May 1993. The NTA has right of approval over foreign investment in Canada's air carriers. The other agency, the Competition Tribunal, first conducted an inquiry as to whether an Air Canada-PWA merger would be anti-competitive, and then debated whether PWA could pull out of Gemini for the CAIL-AMR deal.

There were also five lawsuits. One concerned PWA's charge that Air Canada had engaged in predatory pricing in 1992 in order to drive Canadian Airlines out of the marketplace. The other four involved PWA's effort to withdraw from Gemini. Of these, one was launched by PWA against its fellow Gemini owners, and the remaining three by those owners, both together and separately, against PWA and Canadian Airlines.

On top of all this, seven unions were involved, with separate locals at each airline. In the 1980s, there had been bitter strikes at both Air Canada and PWA, but in 1992 and 1993 the unions aligned themselves with management in order to save the airlines. In addition to the seven unions, an umbrella group was formed by PWA employees expressly to save their company.

One of the unfortunate aspects of the crisis was the shattering of traditional union solidarity as the locals at one airline fought to save their jobs at the expense of those at the other. The parent organizations stayed aloof

James Richardson, the "Father of Canadian Aviation." He established Western Canada Airways, a forerunner of CP Air.
(Canada's Aviation Hall of Fame)

Sir Edward Beatty (1877-1943). He created Canadian Pacific Airlines in 1942 when he was chairman of Canadian Pacific .
(John Boyd/The Globe & Mail)

C.D. Howe, Canada's first minister of transport. He played a key role in the creation of Trans-Canada Air Lines (now Air Canada) in 1937.
(Canadian Press)

Grant McConachie, president of Canadian Pacific Airlines from 1947 to 1965, the year in which he died.
(Canada's Aviation Hall of Fame)

Gordon McGregor, president, TCA/Air Canada, 1948-1968. (TCA was renamed Air Canada in 1964.)
(Canada's Aviation Hall of Fame)

Russell Baker, founder of Pacific Western Airlines. He died in 1958.
(Canada's Aviation Hall of Fame)

Yves Pratte, chairman of Air Canada from 1968-1975.
(Canadian Press)

*Donald Watson, president, PWA,
from 1970-1976.*
(Canada's Aviation Hall of Fame)

*Ian Gray, president, CP Air,
1976-1982.*
(The Globe & Mail)

Ian Sinclair, general solicitor, Canadian Pacific. He represented CP Air when it obtained its first transcontinental route in 1958. He later became president, CEO and chairman of CP, and also chairman of CP Air from 1969-1982.
(John McNeill/The Globe & Mail)

Claude Taylor, who has been with Air Canada since 1949. He became president and CEO, then chairman, and is now chairman emeritus.
(Ed Regan/The Globe & Mail)

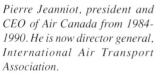

Jean Corbeil, minister of transport (1991-1993) during much of the airline crisis.
(Ed Regan/The Globe & Mail)

Pierre Jeanniot, president and CEO of Air Canada from 1984-1990. He is now director general, International Air Transport Association.
(The Globe & Mail)

Hollis Harris, current chairman, president and CEO of Air Canada.
(Peter Tym/The Globe & Mail)

Max Ward, founder and longtime president of Wardair, which PWA bought in 1989.
(The Globe & Mail)

Donald Carty, executive vice-president of AMR Corporation, in charge of AMR's proposed investment in Canadian Airlines international. He was president, CP Air, 1985-1987, when PWA bought it.
(Erik Christensen/The Globe & Mail)

Rhys Eyton, current chairman, president and CEO of PWA, and also chairman and CEO of Canadian Airlines International.
(Fred Lum/ The Globe & Mail)

Kevin Jenkins, current president of Canadian Airlines International.
(ED Regan/The Globe & Mail)

with the exception of the Canadian Auto Workers Union which represents reservation agents. But its efforts to maintain unity were fiercely attacked by its locals at each airline. So upset were some members that they called union president Basil (Buzz) Hargrove "Mister," the ultimate insult since the usual form of address by unionists is "Brothers" and "Sisters."

The chief winners in the Air Canada-PWA fight have been the lawyers hired by each company. The airlines refuse to disclose how much they have spent on legal fees; all that a PWA board member will say is that it is "a large sum." Considering that many top lawyers were involved in the airlines' numerous legal battles against one another, millions of dollars were undoubtedly paid at the very time that Air Canada and PWA needed every penny to cover operating expenses. PWA has said it has spent substantially in excess of $100 million on "restructuring" costs for such items as legal and advisory fees and settlements with creditors.

Air Canada had two survival strategies – decrease costs, increase revenues. Its cost-saving measures included a 30-percent reduction in employees between 1989 and the end of 1993, relocation of its corporate headquarters from downtown Montreal to its technical centre at Dorval Airport, the sale of its enRoute credit card business for $282 million to Citibank, and the sale and leaseback of a number of planes. The advantage of sale-leasebacks is that they bring in millions of dollars in the short term, while rental payments are spread out over twelve or more years. In 1993 alone, Air Canada made $540 million from the sale and leaseback of seven planes in two transactions. The first was with six international banks, including the Canadian Imperial Bank of Commerce, and the second with General Electric Capital Corporation. Other cost-saving measures were undertaken in its cargo services and its airport ramp operations.

Air Canada's plan to increase revenues through a full or partial merger with Canadian Airlines failed, but other revenue-enhancing strategies did succeed. It purchased a 27.2 percent interest in Continental Airlines, the fifth-largest U.S. airline, and formed a commercial alliance with United Airlines, the second-largest, in which they cooperate on schedules and frequent-flier programs. In addition, Air Canada signed a marketing agreement with Swissair, and arranged a code-sharing agreement with Air France.

Air Canada also expanded its regional airline operations into the United States in an effort to increase revenues. In August 1993, it bought twenty-four planes with a seating capacity of fifty for delivery in 1994, with an option for two dozen more. The jets will be used on routes with enough traffic to fill them but insufficient business to warrant the use of bigger aircraft. Another advantage is that no government approval is necessary for cross-border flights by aircraft with fewer than sixty seats.

But while cost-cutting in many areas, Air Canada elected to spend $22 million on a three-year corporate redesign, beginning in late 1993. This included repainting its planes, issuing new uniforms, and printing new stationery letterhead and baggage tags. For many years, Air Canada's planes have been white with red and burgundy horizontal lines on the body and a white maple leaf in relief against a red tail. The body will now be white, the tail dark green, and the maple leaf red. (All-white is also used on the plane bodies of Continental Airlines of which Air Canada became a part-owner earlier in 1993, and of which Air Canada's chairman Hollis Harris was chief executive before joining Air Canada.) Although there are many Canadian design firms, the redesign was developed by an American firm specializing in airlines' appearances.

Harris explained that the new look is to emphasize both that the airline no longer is government-owned and that it is an "airline for all of Canada, not just Eastern Canada," where Air Canada is headquartered. He maintained the transformation would attract enough additional Western Canadian customers to offset the cost. However, consumers generally care more about service and fares than cosmetics. The redecorating expense seems unwarranted at a time when Air Canada has laid off thousands of workers and slashed the wages of those still in its employ. Moreover, just three weeks before announcing the redesign, it reported a nine-month loss, to September 30, 1993, of $236 million.

PWA's fight to survive began with many cost-saving measures. It reduced the expense of pilot training by one-third, improved baggage-handling procedures, reduced maintenance cycle time and sold twelve planes to airlines in Asia. In 1993, it cancelled purchase commitments for two planes and deferred deliveries of ten, at a total penalty cost of $59.9 million – a substantial sum but less than the purchase price of some types of planes. In addition, Canadian Airlines International reduced its staff by 2,000 from 1989, and Canadian Regional Airlines laid off 1,200 between 1991 and the end of 1993.

Nevertheless, as early as mid-summer 1990, PWA's executives realized the company would require financial restructuring in order to stay alive. But it was not until a year later that an investment dealer was hired to find a prospective investor. Only two firms were interested – Air Canada and AMR. Air Canada proposed a full or partial merger. AMR proposed making a substantial equity investment and providing a broad range of management services on a long-term basis. PWA began discussions with both in the fall of 1991, code-naming its discussions with AMR "Project Iceberg."

A third option could have been chosen – court-imposed creditor protection. PWA did stop paying most of its creditors on November 29, 1992, but kept its promise to resume five months later. Its reason for not seeking court protection was that it had many foreign creditors; Canadian protection would have had no impact in Japan and Europe. Canadian Airlines regularly flies equipment worth $100 million-plus on these routes, and it wanted to avoid having its planes seized by foreign creditors for default.

PWA's ultimate survival plan has three components. The first two involve the issue of 1 billion new common shares, a substantial dilution for existing shareholders since previously PWA had 48 million comon shares. They will be compensated with extra shares for every one already held. Of the 1 billion new shares, 754 million are a debt-for-equity exchange whereby $732 million of debt will be converted. Another 250 million shares are being issued to employees in return for their investment of $200 million through payroll deductions. They also obtained the right to appoint two representatives to PWA's board and one to Canadian's.

The third component of PWA's survival plan is a "strategic alliance" with AMR, which has three elements. The first entails a $246-million investment by AMR in CAIL in return for a one-third economic and 25 percent voting interest, the maximum foreign investment allowed in Canada's airlines. CAIL was selected rather than PWA because Alberta legislation limits individual shareholdings in PWA to 10 percent, whereas no such restriction applies to CAIL.

The second element is a marketing agreement providing reciprocal frequent-flier privileges so that mileage compiled on Canadian and American can be applied to the other.

The third element is a twenty-year services contract under which CAIL will pay AMR an estimated $100 million a year for access to a wide variety of AMR management systems including accounting, data processing, operations planning and pricing. Consequently, AMR will earn back its $246 million investment in CAIL in little more than two years, and make $2 billion all told.

The employees will own 24.9 percent of PWA and then 18.7 percent on a fully diluted basis when the warrants related to the restructuring plan's share issue are drawn down. Their contributions, to be over a four-year period, began in early 1993, and the shareholders approved the debt restructuring in August of that year. Nonetheless, the issue of new shares to both groups was delayed because it was tied to the completion of the strategic alliance with AMR. While the marketing arrangement began on February 1, 1993, a little over a month after the alliance was agreed upon December 29, 1992, the rest of the alliance terms were scheduled to take effect after CAIL transferred the hosting of its internal reservations system, Pegasus, from Gemini to AMR's Sabre, and after gaining government regulatory approval. The National Transportation Agency approved AMR's investment in May 1993, but the Gemini issue dragged on throughout 1993 and into 1994 as Air Canada and Gemini sought to prevent PWA's withdrawal.

As time passed, it became a cliffhanger as to whether PWA would have enough money to survive until the conflict was resolved, and also as to whether AMR would wait for it to be. But whenever the date drew near that PWA had predicted it would run out of cash, it said it had enough for a few more months. Also, AMR gave a number of deadline extensions.

In addition to its stipulation that CAIL switch to Sabre, AMR asked PWA to shift Canadian Regional Airlines from a subsidiary of PWA to Canadian Airlines so that AMR would have an ownership stake in every PWA airline, and they would all purchase its contract services. PWA, however, maintains it had already intended to convert all its operating divisions, including its vacation tour companies, to subsidiaries of Canadian Airlines "to simplify corporate structure as part of our restructuring plan." PWA owns two tour companies – Canadian Holidays, Canada's largest leisure travel tour operator with 497,000 customers in 1992, and Transpacific Tours which markets and provides ground services for overseas visitor tour packages to Canada.

Since the restructuring will limit PWA's holdings to its interest in Canadian Airlines, it raises the question of the need for a separate PWA identity. There appears to be an internal division of opinion. Peter Wallis, CAIL's vice-president, government and regulatory affairs, says: "PWA will continue as the parent company, with a separate board and officers overseeing Canadian. PWA is publicly traded, whereas CAIL isn't. There are holding companies of all sizes in the business world, and PWA will be among the larger ones."

By contrast, Murray Sigler, a member of PWA's board and of its restructuring committee until late 1993, says that PWA could cease to exist because "with the holdings limited to CAIL shares, it becomes a duplicate corporate structure." However, he points out that amending legislation would be necessary because PWA is the legal entity under which the company was incorporated in Alberta. Also, PWA shares would have to be converted into CAIL ones and CAIL become publicly traded.

* * *

There are many reasons why Air Canada and PWA lost so much money from 1990 through 1992. Some of their troubles were unavoidable – the worldwide recession and the Persian Gulf War caused a sharp drop in air travel. High Canadian tax rates were another problem. Other difficulties were self-inflicted – overexpansion, overemployment, and executive-suite turmoil at Air Canada. Both companies experienced difficulties with their regional airlines caused by loose control. Moreover, they were embroiled in a lawsuit over ownership of one of them. Another major problem – over-capacity – was due to a combination of their own mistakes, the weak economy and deregulation. In addition, the industry suffered from the lack of a clearcut government policy. Instead, the government fluctuated be-tween the two extremes of interference and aloofness.

Although the Gulf War adversely affected airline travel in the United States as well as in Canada, U.S. air carriers fared far better financially in 1991 than those in Canada, mainly because of the imposition of the Goods and Services Tax (GST) on January 1, 1991. The GST applies to domestic and Canada-continental U.S. flights by Canadian carriers, but not to other international flights. In addition, the federal government collects an air transportation tax on all flights.

The combined effect of these two taxes was to add about 20 percent to the price of a $200 ticket, 16 percent to a $500 ticket, and 11 percent to a $1,000 ticket – the higher the fare, the lower the tax is as a percentage of the total. In many cases, the taxes alone are equivalent to what fares were many years ago. For example, full round-trip economy fare between Toronto and Ottawa without taxes is $390, with taxes, $457.21; between Toronto and Montreal $246 and $498.43; and between Toronto and Vancouver $1,460 and $1,609.28. Even on discount fares, the taxes push up the price con-siderably; for example, from $193 to $231.67 round-trip between Toronto and Ottawa.

The higher taxes hurt Canada's airlines in two ways: they reduced de-mand and caused the diversion to U.S. carriers of transborder traffic and domestic Canadian traffic originating from and destined for points near the U.S. border. Canada's airlines operate under the additional burdens of higher fuel taxes and weather-related expenses, such as de-icing fluid. Also, they paid substantially higher borrowing costs until the recent drop in Canadian interest rates to a level below those in the U.S. (Canadians flying to the United States also must pay a number of U.S. taxes: immigration, departure and, as of 1994, Customs clearance.)

The problem of overcapacity stems from the nature of the airline indus-try. "It is a capital intensive industry in which fleet upgrade and replace-ment programs are never-ending," says Ted Larkin. But it is difficult for airline executives to calculate precisely how many planes to order because much can happen in the two years it takes to build a plane. Airlines cannot forecast demand for longer than ninety days in advance due to their lack of control over the impact of economic conditions on personal disposable income. Airline industry analyst Tony Hine of investment dealer ScotiaMcLeod jokes that the ideal solution would be "a one-size-fits-all accordion plane which shortens when demand is slow and stretches for peak times."

In the air travel boom years of the late 1980s, airlines worldwide had high hopes of continuing good fortune in the 1990s. Air Canada committed itself to spending $3.8 billion by 1994 and Canadian to $1.6 billion. As they saw it, they had good reasons for their purchases in addition to their expectations of a high volume of passenger traffic. They regarded the new planes principally as fleet renewal rather than expansion. Although planes have a physical life of as long as fifty years, aircraft under ten years old are the backbone of modern airlines, close to the average age of both Canadian's and Air Canada's fleets. (The life of a plane is measured in terms of hours flown and the number of takeoff and landing cycles. Typically, it takes twenty to twenty-five years for a plane to fly 80,000 to 100,000 hours and 40,000 to 50,000 cycles, although planes that fly shorter routes tend to age more quickly because their takeoff and landing cycles occur more frequently.) Thus, strictly speaking, it was not the new planes that created Air Canada's and Canadian's overcapacity problems but their older planes which they could not sell owing to the glut of aircraft worldwide. Moreover, Air Canada and Canadian characterized the investment as partly a cost-cutting measure seeing that the new planes would require only two pilots as compared to the three necessary for older planes. To allow for workshifts, each plane must have six sets of pilots; thus, the new planes needed six fewer pilots than the older aircraft. Considering that pilots' salaries range up to $100,000 a year at both companies, the smaller cockpit crews produce substantial savings.

The aircraft orders were a major reason why the long-term debt, as well as aircraft capital lease obligations of both companies doubled between 1988 and 1992. Unfortunately for Air Canada and Canadian, by the time deliveries began passenger traffic had dropped substantially due to the onset of the recession in 1990 and the compounded impact of the 1991 Persian Gulf War. Air passenger traffic in Canada fell by 15 percent in 1991.

This decline, combined with the delivery of new planes, caused the two airlines severe overcapacity problems averaging 20 percent; on some routes which had back-to-back flights, the percentage was far higher. For instance, in the summer of 1992 Air Canada and Canadian Airlines combined flew fifteen flights a day westbound from Toronto to Vancouver with a total of 2,860 seats, even though traffic in preceding years was only 1,250. Moreover, many of their departure times were a mere five minutes apart; even the longest period between flights was only forty-five minutes.

The overcapacity problem contributed to operating expenses exceeding operating revenues at both companies in 1991 and 1992. No longer could they rely on the appreciation in value of their aircraft and their subsequent sale to boost their results. For example, between 1983 and 1988, the year they began placing their massive aircraft orders, 67 percent of PWA's profit and 63 percent of Air Canada's came from the sale of planes. "They made more money trading aluminum than flying planes," says Tony Hine. But since 1990, aircraft values have fallen by as much as 40 percent. Thus, the airlines can no longer rely on plane sales to prop up their results.

While there is agreement on the dimensions of the overcapacity problem, there is dissension as to the causes. The Mulroney government insisted that the industry was solely at fault. But, the government's deregulation policy was also responsible.

Based on experience gained as recently as the 1981-82 recession, the airlines should have known better. For example, in 1981-82, Pierre Jeanniot, then executive vice-president and chief of airline operations at Air Canada, had grounded the airline's least efficient planes. Now director general of the International Air Transport Association, which represents airlines around the world, Jeanniot says: "More airlines should have done this with their inefficient planes between 1990 and 1992. It would have reduced the overcapacity problem." He goes on to criticize his former employer's choice of jumbo jets to ground during the current crisis. "It is really hard to understand why Air Canada chose in 1991-92 to park its brand-new and efficient 747-400s while flying the rather inefficient old 747-100s," he says.

Air Canada and PWA did not meet the conventional benchmark of an 8 percent operating margin (operating income as a percentage of revenue) as to whether airlines can afford new equipment. Air Canada has never achieved a margin greater than 5 percent. PWA, which had margins exceeding 8 percent in six years during the 1980s, has not had satisfactory operating margins since 1987, the year it bought CP Air.

There were additional warning signals about overcapacity. "Everybody — airlines, manufacturers, lenders — should have known it was coming well in advance," says John Eichner, chairman, Simat, Helliesen and Eichner, a New York aviation consulting firm. For example, he says airline executives should have learned that "the industry is highly sensitive to recessions which are influenced by outside events." If they had, Eichner says the airlines might have been better prepared to cope with the impact of the Persian Gulf War on the economic recession.

Another sign, he continues, was the increase in the number of aircraft that were not being flown or were being offered for sale at low prices. "Since 1991, there have been over nine hundred old and new aircraft available for sale," he states. "Moreover, out of the seven hundred-plus aircraft parked by airlines from around the world in the desert in the U.S. Southwest, well over one hundred are the newest generation equipment." The Southwest is chosen because the dry climate preserves planes well.

In addition, Eichner says that experience should also have taught the airlines that, because of the time needed for production, there is a two-year span between the peak for orders and the peak for deliveries. "Thus, a peak in orders is an early warning signal of when excess capacity will occur," he points out.

Airlines worldwide ignored all the signals, not just Air Canada and PWA. They also decided to handle this crisis differently from the past. Traditionally, when traffic declined, the airlines had maintained prices in an effort to sustain profits from the business they still had. Now, however, they engaged in price wars to hold onto market share or pump up business. "The artificial growth caused them to lose their collective shirts," Eichner says. Between 1990 and 1992, the world's 213 major airlines lost U.S.$9 billion, more than all the profits they made in the 1980s.

Yet, while the airlines were losing money due to their price wars, consumers were not deriving much benefit from the lower fares for several reasons. First, the price wars were sporadic. Second, full economy, business and first-class fares have increased under deregulation at a pace greater than the inflation rate. For example, round-trip full economy fare (excluding taxes) between Toronto and Montreal has risen from $350 in 1990 to $426 in 1993 (a 21.7 percent increase); between Toronto and Ottawa from $304 to $390 (28.3 percent increase); and between Toronto and Vancouver from $1,184 to $1,460 (23 percent increase). By contrast, the consumer price index rose by 11.3 percent between 1990 and the end of 1992.

Nevertheless, the airlines' yields (revenue per seat mile[1]) – the most revealing figure as to how well airlines are doing – have declined since 1986 in non-inflationary terms. The reason for the decline is that the number of people travelling on discount fares has increased markedly. About two-thirds of all air tickets sold to Canadians are at discount prices compared to 64 percent in 1990 and 54 percent in 1987. Thus, when critics say the airlines should raise fares to improve profits they are referring primarily to the discounts. But consumers retort that discount fares are less of a bargain than they were in their early days because the size of discounts has decreased under deregulation. According to the most recent figures available, the average discount on the most travelled twenty-five city-to-city routes in Canada was equal to 30 percent of the standard economy fare in 1991,

---

[1] See Appendix II, p. 164.

down from the peak discount levels of about 35 percent in 1987 and 1988 when deregulation officially started.

These statistics come from the report of the National Transportation Act Review Commission, which was released in early 1993. The Commission was established to assess the impact of the 1987 National Transportation Act. The report as well as the Conservative governments of Brian Mulroney and Kim Campbell insisted that the airlines were solely responsible for the overcapacity problem. Time and again Jean Corbeil, transport minister under both Mulroney and Campbell, maintained that "the airlines know what their problem is. It is overcapacity. If they know what the problem is, they should attack it themselves."

The National Transportation Act Review Commission took the same stand. "Economic regulatory reform did not cause the current state of the industry. The airlines put themselves in their current position," it said in almost the same words as Corbeil repeatedly used. Of course, considering that the Act had established deregulation in Canada, it would have been extraordinary for the Commission to blame deregulation for the airlines' troubles. It also would have been extraordinary for Mulroney, Campbell and Corbeil to repudiate the Conservatives' policy.

However, under the old regulatory process the overcapacity problem likely would not have been as severe because the federal government set the number of flights per day, thereby limiting capacity. Under deregulation, the number of flights and types of planes used are determined solely by market forces. Because the airlines' natural goal is to increase market share, under deregulation they added flights and seat capacity in the hope that enlarged supply would increase demand, although the conventional wisdom is that demand should exceed supply for business success.

Neither airline was willing to cut back for fear of losing market share to the other. Therefore, they asked the federal government to order reductions in capacity. Corbeil refused to do so, saying once again that they "should attack the problem themselves." But it was not until the summer of 1993 that both airlines reduced capacity by 11 percent, thus only partially relieving the problem.

As for overexpansion, the problem is not confined to the airline industry. The big question for all businesspeople is how much growth is wise: too little and their business will stagnate; too much and it will become overextended and perhaps collapse. There have been many recent examples of Canadian businesses not knowing when to pause, most notably Olympia & York Developments, until then one of the world's leading real estate developers. From the outset, Canada's airline industry has been characterized by a desire to grow – from charter to scheduled, from local to regional, from regional to national, and from national to global.

In the case of Canada's two major airlines, PWA's objective was to expand from a regional to a national and international airline. Therefore, it bought CP Air and Wardair. Air Canada, which had been a national and international airline from its beginning, wanted to become one of the world's leading global carriers. That is why it added what analysts say were too many international destinations before deciding it would be better to expand around the world through acquiring all of Canadian Airlines or, failing that, its international routes. When it was unable to get either all or part of Canadian, Air Canada formed its equity alliance with Continental Airlines and its non-equity, commercial arrangement with United Airlines.

"Before PWA bought CP Air and Wardair, it was a consistently profitable regional airline. Between 1986 and 1991, it quadrupled in size and went from consistent profits with a conservative balance sheet to consistent losses and excess leverage," says Tony Hine. "As for Air Canada, it had a vision of becoming a global carrier. That vision took it on a five-year fantasy ride from Toronto to London, Bombay and Singapore." The "fantasy ride" was one reason Air Canada ordered more planes and, when the anticipated traffic did not materialize, its overcapacity problem was aggravated.

Thousands of workers at both airlines have lost their jobs since 1989 because the airlines' profitability and survival depend chiefly on how well they contain costs. Seeing that they have no control over plane prices, taxes, interest rates, government landing fees, airport terminal charges and check-in counter-space rents, the airlines have focused on lowering labour costs as a way to slash expenses.

Wage rates are governed by contracts with the various unions covering pilots, reservation agents, flight attendants, machinists, baggage handlers, airline dispatchers, flight simulator technologists and clerical service workers. Both unionized workers and management agreed to wage freezes and then wage cuts as Air Canada's and PWA's conditions worsened. In addition to these measures, both airlines – particularly Air Canada – lowered their labour costs by laying off many of their employees. Canadian's employment has declined annually by the hundreds – from 16,500 in 1989 to 14,600 in 1993. Air Canada's workforce has decreased each year by several thousand – from 23,200 in 1989 to 16,000 in 1993.

Air Canada's labour productivity – output per worker – has consistently been less than that of Canadian Airlines and major U.S. airlines. In 1992, its productivity was 20 percent less than Canadian's and close to 30 percent less than that at American Airlines and United Airlines. Air Canada maintains that these figures are an unfair comparison because it does more contract work for other airlines while at the same time sub-contracting less.

Analysts concede that some of the difference is related to how much maintenance is done in-house. But, they say that even with this taken into account, Air Canada was way behind in productivity. "Air Canada says comparing labour productivity is a game of comparing apples and oranges because of its ancillary revenue from labour-intensive operations such as ground handling. But the real problem was not apples and oranges; it was that Air Canada had too many mandarins," puns Tony Hine about Air Canada's excessive number of middle managers until recently.

When Air Canada's management ranks were at their most bloated, its bankers were known to complain that more Air Canada people turned up for meetings than from the bank. At government hearings, there were often more Air Canada than government representatives. At one National Transportation Agency session, Air Canada had a person from each province to underscore its point that all of Canada was affected. An NTA member, however, regarded the number as excessive. "You have ten people doing the job of one," he said.

When Hollis Harris joined Air Canada as vice-chairman, president and chief executive officer in February 1992, one of his priorities was to purge Air Canada's Crown corporation mentality which had remained alive and well despite privatization being completed three years earlier. Harris said he found three people doing the job of one. While admitting that the Crown corporation mentality took a long time to shake off, Claude Taylor, chairman at the time privatization began, points out that "no airline has been able to downsize as fast as the market has." But, as he also says, Air Canada "had more to do than most airlines."

It was difficult for Air Canada to make the transition from the mentality of a government-owned corporation to that of private enterprise because about 75 percent of its staff had worked for it for fifteen years or longer. Thus, making the adjustment in mindset took a while for some. James Tennant, executive vice-president of human resources from 1992 until he left in 1993 after twenty-six years with the company, compares the process to learning to swim: "Theory and classroom instruction are not enough; pool experience is essential," he stresses.

Although Air Canada had more employees than needed, Pierre Jeanniot, who as president and CEO from 1984 to 1990 tried to reduce this featherbedding, points out that "all large corporations – not just Air Canada – tend to be bureaucratic." He goes on to say that one reason for Air Canada's high employment numbers was that being a Crown corporation, it needed the people to provide all the information demanded from it. "The government requested lots of data and details; members of Parliament had their own ideas on how the airline should be run; and I had to appear before

Parliamentary Committees and Commissions not just regarding transport matters, but also about a wide range of other issues – such as languages – about which they wanted to know what Air Canada did," he recalls.

Still, Jeanniot concedes that Air Canada did suffer from a Crown-corporation complex. He personally tried to combat it, beginning in 1970 with his first vice-presidential appointment. "In a Crown corporation bureaucracy, people tend to write letters to one another, rather than talk, even though they may be as close as the next office," he says. "Therefore, I told my staff that they were to speak to one another and were only to write memos about very serious matters. To underline how strongly I felt, I said I would get rid of those who did otherwise." Subsequently, when he became chief operating officer, Jeanniot invited the company's vice-presidents to drop in daily between 8:15 and 8:45 a.m. for informal discussions over a cup of coffee from a percolator in his office. He continued this practice as chief executive officer so as "to encourage the free flow of ideas."

Air Canada's difficulties in shedding its Crown corporation mentality and grappling with its financial problems were compounded by executive-suite turbulence created by Jeanniot's abrupt resignation in August 1990. Jeanniot, who had been president and CEO for six years, was then fifty-seven years old and had been with Air Canada for thirty-five years.

Conflicting reasons were given as to why he left. An Air Canada spokesperson gave a rather weak explanation: "He has been president for six years and it's a big job. He's probably met the personal goals he had as president." Observers outside Air Canada said Jeanniot quit over losing a dispute with Air Canada's board over how Air Canada's workforce should be decreased. They thought he advocated attrition and had promised the unions there would be no layoffs, a reversal of his stand five years earlier when the issue also arose – but that the board of directors overruled him.

There was some truth to both explanations. Jeanniot did think that after a certain number of years "there is a question of whether a CEO still has something to offer." However, he regarded eight years as the proper point of departure and in 1990 he had been CEO for only six years. As for the layoffs, he believed they would not be necessary if more "productivity were extracted from growth of the business."

But the real reason Jeanniot quit was that he had lost the power struggle between himself and Claude Taylor over who was actually chief executive officer – Jeanniot, who then occupied the position, or Taylor, who had held it just prior. "A company can't have more than one chief executive officer," Jeanniot says.

The Jeanniot-Taylor conflict broke into the open shortly after Jeanniot succeeded Taylor in 1984 as president and CEO, and revolved around the issue of labour costs. During the 1982 recession, Taylor, as CEO, had chosen not to resort to mass layoffs as a way to cut costs. While his refusal was compassionate and enhanced his popularity among employees, it had negative repercussions – heavier losses than Air Canada would otherwise have sustained. Moreover, these losses were the highest to date in Air Canada's history.

Shortly after Jeanniot became CEO, the 1985 recession began and he was convinced "tough measures were essential for the survival of the company." Principally, he believed labour costs should be decreased from 35 percent of total expenditures to 29 percent. That is the level at which they are today. To achieve this goal, he imposed a wage freeze in conjunction with longer working hours, eliminated more than four hundred management positions through a voluntary retirement plan, and wiped out one-third of the senior vice-presidential positions.

Air Canada was by no means alone in demanding concessions from its workers in the mid-1980s. All airlines were doing so to offset the lower revenues they were making due to the recession and the discount fares of de facto deregulation. Jeanniot says Air Canada "needed more concessions than the private airlines."

The demands for worker concessions sparked protest strikes at all the airlines, but Air Canada had the most – three. In 1985 its flight attendants went on strike for twenty-four days between April and May, and for forty-seven days between August and October. In December 1987, during the usually lucrative Christmas travel season, it was shut down for three weeks by a machinists and baggage handlers strike. Jeanniot stood firm through all three strikes, wanting to impress upon the unions that "When I said no, I meant no," because he believed that in order for Air Canada "to regain productivity lost in past negotiations, significant changes inconveniencing some people" had to be made. Improving Air Canada's productivity was crucial for the airline to achieve its goal of privatization. It urgently needed to strengthen its balance sheet so as to be an attractive investment to stock market investors.

Jeanniot says Claude Taylor was not supportive of him because he disliked strikes; as president, he had experienced a twelve-day strike in 1978, the company's last labour dispute prior to those in 1985. But after the 1987 strike, other differences of opinion arose between them over Jeanniot's expansionist plans. Jeanniot was convinced the best way to improve Air Canada's bottom line was to increase productivity through business growth. He also thought Air Canada needed to develop a greater international presence, particularly in Asia to which its rival, Canadian Airlines, had been flying since 1949.

Thus, he began the Air Canada flights to Singapore and Bombay, a move which prompted analyst Tony Hine's harsh "fantasy ride" criticism. Jeanniot also intended to begin Air Canada flights to the Philippines, Malaysia and Korea. In his view, all these new flights were not a foolish "fantasy ride," but sound business. He foresaw them generating revenue from both passengers and cargo.

Regarding passengers, he explains that air travellers can be divided into three categories: businesspeople, vacationers and people who go back to their roots. "The original roots of Canada were European and in Air Canada's earlier days much of its international traffic was derived from people travelling across the Atlantic," he says. "But the new roots of Canadians were in Asia and India to a great extent and, therefore, there was a large potential market in this direction for Air Canada." As for Singapore, Jeanniot believed Air Canada should fly there because Singapore is a major Far Eastern business centre.

Realizing that there would not likely be enough people, however, to fill a jumbo jet on these flights, Jeanniot planned to reconfigure the planes designated for these routes so that half the space could be set aside for cargo, a practice followed by European airlines. "North American airlines pay relatively little attention to cargo, whereas European ones tend to integrate passenger and cargo service," he points out. "For example, KLM Royal Dutch Airlines derives 25 percent of its revenues from freight. I thought this strategy was applicable to Air Canada because its routes did not have the density of population that those of U.S. airlines had." On average, Air Canada makes 10 percent of its revenue from cargo. Also, as part of his vision of converting Air Canada into a global carrier, Jeanniot began discussing commercial alliances with Air France, Korean Airlines and US Air.

Besides adding routes and negotiating alliances, Jeanniot diversified Air Canada into non-airline businesses to increase revenue. He acquired a number of courier delivery services. He also aggressively promoted Air Canada's enRoute credit card which he had relaunched in 1979 with $1 million in new computer programming when he became senior vice-president of marketing and planning. He believed the diversification would benefit Air Canada because "the airline business itself is seldom very profitable. More profits can often be made from peripheral businesses. For example, in many years 40 percent or more of American Airlines' profit has come from its Sabre reservation system. Further, it has been said that Pan American might not have disappeared if it had sold its airline rather than its other businesses, such as its hotels."

Whether due to or despite Jeanniot's expansionism, Air Canada's profits increased every year between 1986 and 1989. But in 1990, as the recession took hold, Air Canada began to pile up losses and questions arose as to whether the unprofitable new routes to Singapore and Bombay should be continued. While in the long run they could become profitable, it could take many years, but probably not the quarter century it had taken CP Air to make money on its route to Sydney, Australia, begun in 1948.

As 1990 moved along, Jeanniot became increasingly unhappy as a number of his decisions were reversed by Air Canada's board of directors. The board's composition had changed since his appointment as CEO in 1984, and as it met only five times a year for just a couple of hours it was "not that knowledgeable," in Jeanniot's opinion. He also came to feel that Claude Taylor "may or may not have orchestrated the reversal of a couple of my decisions." In his view, Taylor was "very ambitious for his own personal glory" to be CEO again. Jeanniot was ambitious, too. After all, without ambition plus ability, neither man would have risen from the lowest to the highest level at Air Canada.

By August 1990, Jeanniot decided to quit. Some of his innovations were dumped; others were retained. Just two months later, in October, Air Canada cancelled its Singapore and Bombay flights as well as ones Jeanniot had started to Athens, Madrid and Lisbon. The company also began to lay off employees. "When I left, the company cut people and product to increase productivity but by cutting routes, it lost clients and revenue," he maintains.

Jeanniot was vindicated in November 1993 when Air Canada reinstated flights between Canada and India, although to New Delhi rather than Bombay. It did so for the very reason Jeanniot had begun them in 1985 – to obtain expatriate business. Also, although Jeanniot does not draw attention to the fact, Air Canada continued to pursue his objective of making itself a global airline through commercial alliances with numerous other airlines in Europe, Asia, the Middle East, the Caribbean and the United States, including its April 1993 purchase of 27.2 percent of Continental Airlines.

Some of the courier services had been sold before Jeanniot left, and the rest were sold afterward. The company made a huge return on its $1-million software investment in its enRoute credit card business when it sold it to Citibank Canada in 1992 for $282 million. Air Canada did sign a commercial alliance with Air France, which became effective in 1993. On the other hand, it lost out regarding US Air; British Airways acquired 25 percent of that airline in 1993.

* * *

In that he is now director general of the International Air Transport Association, Jeanniot has done well in the airline industry since his departure from Air Canada. For eighteen months after he left, Taylor, who turned sixty-five in 1990, resumed the positions of president and chief executive officer, while continuing to serve as chairman. He says that there was nobody "ready in the company" to succeed him because one person he had groomed as a successor was "lost due to medical reasons and others had been attracted away by other companies." When a successor was found, it was not someone from Air Canada but rather an outsider and an American – Hollis Harris.

"We had gone outside the company on occasion before when the skills were not available in Canada," Taylor says. His remark could also be construed as a devastating comment on the calibre of talent at Air Canada or as a reluctance to promote from within.

Harris was not Air Canada's first choice. It had initially offered the position to Donald Carty, a Canadian who had been president of CP Air before becoming executive vice-president of American Airlines. However, they were unable to come to terms over money. Also, Carty is said by some airline analysts to have suggested moving Air Canada's headquarters to Toronto. If so, the idea would have arisen largely from the fact that Pearson International Airport handles the most passenger traffic in Canada. However, such a move would have triggered a political and public relations uproar. The upshot is that Air Canada has an American as its president, and American Airlines has a Canadian as the executive vice-president in charge of negotiating American's investment in Canadian Airlines, Air Canada's chief rival.

Hollis Harris, born in 1931 in Georgia, speaks with a pronounced southern accent. An aeronautical engineer, he worked for thirty-three years at Delta Air Lines, the third-largest U.S. airline, becoming its president in 1987. In August 1990, he became chairman of Continental Airlines. Continental, which was already in severe financial trouble, filed for bankruptcy protection in December of the same year, and in August 1991 Harris was forced to resign. Taylor says it was "best for Air Canada to obtain someone with international experience to bridge the period." Harris will not be sixty-five until November 1996 and by then Air Canada should have been able to groom a successor from within its ranks.

In addition to the problems in their main business, Air Canada and PWA became involved in a struggle in 1990 and 1991 to acquire Air Toronto, a commuter airline operating between Toronto and a number of U.S. cities. Established in 1984 by a firm called Soundair, Air Toronto had become an Air Canada connector in 1987, feeding traffic into Air Canada at Pearson International Airport. In April 1990, just twenty-two days before Soundair went into receivership, Air Canada offered to buy Air Toronto for $18 million.

Two months later, Air Canada lowered its offer to $8.2 million and terminated its contractual arrangement with Air Toronto when the court-appointed Soundair receiver, the firm of Ernst & Young, did not accept the offer on behalf of Air Toronto. Convinced that Air Toronto required a connector arrangement to stay alive, Ernst & Young first contacted a number of U.S. airlines it thought would be interested because of Air Toronto's transborder routes. Since they all declined, Ernst & Young approached PWA which referred it to Ontario Express, PWA's Ontario regional airline.

On February 8, 1991, Ontario Express offered $2 million cash and an additional amount by way of a share of the gross revenue of Air Toronto. On March 7, one of Air Toronto's two major creditors, supported by Air Canada, made a counter-offer. However, the next day Ernst & Young accepted the Ontario Express offer since it believed the sole purpose of the counter-offer "was to interrupt the finalizing of the Ontario Express agreement and to retain as long as possible the Air Toronto connector traffic for the benefit of Air Canada."

An appeal against this ruling was made to the Ontario Court of Justice's General Division which rejected it. While Justice Alvin Rosenberg conceded that the counter-offer was "superior" in terms of money, he said the difference was "not of such a magnitude as to warrant the disruption" of the sale to Ontario Express. He further stated that Ernst & Young was correct in accepting Ontario Express's offer because it "was looking at a fully baked loaf of bread versus some dough that possibly could be fashioned into a loaf of bread that might be marginally superior."

It was also during 1991 that Air Canada and PWA formed their regional holding companies – Air Canada Regional Holdings and Canadian Regional Airlines – to achieve more cohesiveness. Both also tried with varying success to gain full ownership of their regionals, although from the outset Air Canada had a majority interest in its five regionals unlike PWA.

Before Air Canada Regional Holdings was established, the commercial managers at its regionals reported to the parent company's marketing and scheduling people and the financial managers to its finance staff. Frequently there was inconsistency between what the two Air Canada groups said, so that the regionals were at a loss as to what course of action to follow. "They wondered if the folks at Air Canada spoke to one another and often felt as if they were explaining Air Canada to Air Canada," says James Tennant, an Air Canada senior vice-president who was made the initial president of Air Canada Regional Holdings. Subsequently, in his final year with Air Canada, he became executive vice-president of human resources.

In addition, there was not a clearly defined relationship between Air Canada and its regionals regarding safety matters. This deficiency was brought to light by the 1989 crash of an Air Ontario plane at Dryden,

Ontario, that killed twenty-seven people. Air Ontario was 75 percent-owned by Air Canada, and the ensuing enquiry found that Air Ontario had a lower level of flight safety than Air Canada.

Besides improving communication between the companies, Air Canada Regional Holdings had the further objective of improving profits through sharing costs. By instituting fleet commonality, it was able to achieve economies of scale in bulk purchasing of planes and parts. In addition, the regionals exchange equipment on occasion. For instance, when the regionals' collision avoidance systems were upgraded, one line lent another aircraft and so on until the work was done for all the regionals. The regionals have slashed their bill for pilot flight simulator training by buying a group block of time.

They also standardized the quality of material and size of uniform shirts as well as the design and size of napkins and drinking glasses, while retaining their individual logos. As a result, the regionals reduced their costs by millions of dollars. In addition to the streamlining benefits, the regionals benefited technologically by "replicating the best demonstrated practice of any one carrier across all of them," according to Darcy Little who became general manager of Air Canada Regional Holdings in 1993.

As well as creating cohesiveness between the regionals, Air Canada Regional Holdings was formed with the intention of Air Canada's acquiring the minority interest in the three regionals it did not fully own – Air Ontario (25 percent minority interest), Air Alliance (also 25 percent), and AirBC (15 percent). Its attempt to buy the rest of Air Ontario triggered a lawsuit. Nothing has been done about Air Alliance or AirBC whose longtime president Iain Harris received a 15 percent interest as a condition of his remaining after the Air Canada takeover.

The Air Ontario case is revealing about Air Canada's tactics. Air Ontario originated in 1961 as Great Lakes Airlines, flying between Toronto and Sarnia, Ontario. In 1985, Air Canada and PWA each bought 24.5 percent. In 1986 Air Canada purchased PWA's shares and the controlling interest of Air Ontario's then major shareholder, the Deluce family, giving Air Canada 75 percent. The Deluces retained 25 percent.

The lawsuit between Deluceco, the Deluces' holding company, and Air Canada arose out of the way Air Canada tried to gain the Deluces's 25 percent interest. Under their shareholdings' agreement, Air Canada was given the option to acquire the Deluces's interest upon the termination of employment of Stanley Deluce, Air Ontario's chairman, and his son, William, the president.

Stanley's two-year contract expired in 1989 and was not renewed. Air Canada Regional Holdings was established in April 1991; in May, president

James Tennant asked William Deluce to resign. William, then forty-two years old, refused but agreed to being replaced as president in return for his being made vice-chairman and chief executive officer. Six days later, he was praised at Air Ontario's board meeting by Air Canada's representative as having "done a superb job in directing the company throughout his tenure as president." Nonetheless, in October 1991, William was removed from his new position of vice-chairman and chief executive officer.

The Deluces charged that in view of the laudatory comments about William's performance, the real reason for his dismissal was that Air Canada wanted to acquire their shares at a lower price than it would otherwise have had to pay. They sought a trial on the grounds that Air Canada had "oppressed" the minority shareholders. Their application was heard by Justice Robert Blair of the Ontario Court's General Division. While he said in his ruling of November 1992 that Air Canada's objective of acquiring all of Air Ontario was "quite legitimate," Blair ordered a trial on the grounds that "Air Canada's conduct may well have been oppressive." He also said that "the evidence strongly supports a conclusion that Air Canada nominees were acting to carry out an Air Canada agenda."

Near the end of 1993, as a trial date loomed, the two sides reached an agreement whereby the Deluces discontinued their lawsuit in return for Air Canada's agreeing to pay an amount, set by arbitration, that would be fairer. The price was not publicly disclosed. William Deluce did not return to the company and Air Canada has achieved its goal of total ownership of Air Ontario.

Whereas Air Canada owned a majority interest in its regionals before forming its regional holding company, PWA had only a minority interest in its five regionals prior to 1991. "We had the cash investment but were getting no cash return; an investment should always be a controlling one," says Murray Sigler, Canadian Regional's first president. Furthermore, there was a lack of fleet commonality as well as of scheduling coordination between the regionals and Canadian Airlines International. Full control of two regionals – Time Air, operating in Western Canada, and Ontario Express – was obtained in early 1991.

Although Air Canada Regional Holdings has centralized purchasing of equipment and uniforms to obtain volume discounts and coordinate marketing, its regionals retain their own names and management. Canadian Regional, however, decided to centralize such functions as human resources, labour relations, corporate planning, corporate communications and service quality at its head office so as to reduce duplication and thus keep down administrative costs. In 1993, Canadian Regional consolidated the 100 percent-owned operations of Time Air and Ontario Express under the Canadian Regional name, and it intended to do the same by year-end with Inter-Canadien, its Quebec regional.

The restructuring led to Russ Eyton, the son of PWA chairman and president Rhys Eyton, losing his job because the marketing department at Ontario Express, in which he was an analyst, no longer was needed. A commerce graduate, Eyton had long been interested in the airline business. Naturally, he could not work for Air Canada. He chose to join Canadian Regional to avoid charges of nepotism that might have arisen if he had worked for PWA at its head office in Calgary. Ontario Express's president Duncan Fischer became Canadian Regional's president when Sigler resigned in June 1993 to start a consulting business.

Just as Air Canada's relationship with Air Ontario became acrimonious, so did Canadian Regional's with one of its airlines – Air Atlantic. Craig Dobbin, Air Atlantic's majority owner, and Canadian Airlines disagreed over the number of St. John's-Halifax-Toronto flights each would operate. Although it cannot settle private industry disputes, the federal Department of Transport did serve as a sort of referee, with the upshot that Air Atlantic obtained more flights. In late 1993 Dobbin bought out PWA's 45-percent interest, but Air Atlantic continues to be part of the Canadian Regional network as a connector.

The relationship with 45 percent-owned Manitoba-based Calm Air International, the fifth regional airline, is harmonious.

* * *

Over and above all their other difficulties, Air Canada and PWA were beset by inconsistent federal government policy which ran the gamut from interference to later dodging the issue.

The government was dragged into the crisis as a result of mounting financial problems at PWA in July 1992. At the beginning of that month, PWA's cash-strapped balance sheet was subjected to conflicting demands. Concerned that PWA would run out of cash before government approval would be obtained for their deal, AMR insisted that PWA add $150 million to its resources. Otherwise, AMR said, it would not sign the agreement whereby it was to invest $246 million in CAIL.

Simultaneously, PWA was under pressure from its directors to establish a liability trust fund for them against claims that could total $105 million in the event of PWA's collapse. Under Canadian law, company directors can be held personally liable for unpaid wages, severance pay, goods and services taxes, and pension plan and unemployment insurance contributions. Considering that PWA only had about $70 to $80 million in cash at the time, it lacked the ready money to fulfill either AMR's or the directors' demands. All it could do was to set aside $40 million in a liability trust fund.

In an effort to ease PWA's cash shortage, its board asked the federal government and those of the three provinces where it had the most employees – Alberta, British Columbia and Ontario – for $215 million to back a proposed $200-million share issue. The provinces refused to help, arguing that the industry's troubles were due to the Mulroney government's deregulation policy and that, therefore, it should take care of the situation.

The government had already promised to assist PWA by buying three jets from it for $150 million. But on July 23 it shocked PWA chairman Rhys Eyton by attaching an ultimatum: it would provide the money only if PWA ended its talks with AMR and resumed those with Air Canada. PWA had terminated merger talks with Air Canada in March after signing a letter of intent with AMR. Although the majority of PWA's board favoured dealing with AMR, under the circumstances they had no choice but to comply with the government. Thus, on July 27, PWA resumed talking to Air Canada. But it did so on a non-exclusive basis and AMR continued to express interest in an alliance.

On the very same day, PWA's directors laid to rest their fears about potential liability by resigning from PWA's wholly-owned subsidiaries including Canadian Airlines International. PWA is a holding company and the subsidiaries its operating divisions. The directors did remain on PWA's board. CAIL's alliance with AMR calls for Canadian to have an eight-member board – six PWA nominees, including the representative employees gained in return for their $200-million investment, and two AMR nominees.

The government's role in making PWA reverse its course was not immediately obvious, especially as Deputy Prime Minister Donald Mazankowski gave no hint of its involvement. "Canadian Airlines chose to try and forge an alliance with AMR. That obviously failed. The only other option is a merger," he said.

However, within days of his statement, the government's strong-arm tactics became public knowledge. Westerners perceived the government's persuasion of PWA as yet another instance of apparent anti-Western Canada, pro-Quebec bias. The controversy was further inflamed by its coinciding with a debate over whether Quebec should be granted more powers under proposed changes to the Constitution.

The government insisted that it was merely acting on the opinion of a longtime PWA director that PWA would go bankrupt if it did not merge with Air Canada. What the government failed to take into account was that his view was shared by only a minority of PWA's directors. The majority preferred an alliance with AMR. The government maintained it was unaware that there were two camps at PWA. Its lack of knowledge is a mystery considering that PWA's rejection back in March of a merger with Air Canada in favour of an alliance with AMR was publicly announced.

However, the government-enforced merger discussions with Air Canada lasted a mere three weeks owing to PWA's employees agreeing on their own initiative to provide PWA with $120 to $150 million through payroll deductions, equivalent to the equity infusion AMR had demanded. PWA's directors accepted their offer on August 14, and on August 17 PWA rejected a merger with Air Canada and revived its attempt to form a link with AMR.

Aggrieved at what it regarded as unjustified criticism of its plan, the government rapidly faded from the scene with the exception of its provision of $50 million in emergency financing to PWA in November 1992. While some at PWA grumbled that the money was only a small portion of the $190 million sought, others approved of the limited assistance. They included Sidney Fattedad, who organized the employee investment plan and was subsequently selected as one of the two employee representatives on PWA's board. "The federal government acted very responsibly," he says. "By only giving $50 million, it forced PWA to acknowledge that it had to restructure its debt."

Aside from the $50 million, the Conservative government dodged the airline crisis in an effort to avoid a repetition of the controversy that had erupted when it took a stand in July 1992. Its position was that the industry should "self-discipline" itself, as Transport Minister Jean Corbeil put it. No matter how hard he was pressed, Corbeil persisted in staying aloof, giving ambiguous answers or none at all. However, Mazankowski was specific during an interview for this book on May 28, 1993, the day after the National Transportation Agency approved AMR's proposed investment in CAIL. He said: "Yes, Canada can sustain two airlines and what both are doing regarding strategic alliances is the right way to go." He was referring to Air Canada's April 1993 investment in Continental Airlines, as well as the proposed AMR-CAIL deal. Thus, as of May 1993 Mazankowski no longer was backing an Air Canada-PWA merger as he had in July 1992 as the answer to PWA's problems.

When Kim Campbell became prime minister in June 1993, she retained Corbeil as transport minister, a clear signal that she agreed with his non-interventionist stand. She also declined to become involved, refusing to appoint a mediator in the Air Canada-CAIL dispute over CAIL's seeking to leave the Gemini computerized reservation system. "That's not what the airlines want," she stated firmly, even though CAIL executives had emphasized repeatedly that it was precisely what they wanted. In a vivid metaphor, Ted Larkin of Bunting Warburg compares the government's standoffish role in the Air Canada-PWA struggle "to the police not stepping in to stop two streetfighters in an alley who are armed with knives."

The Liberals' position for many months was that the government should appoint a blue-ribbon panel to review the situation and make recommendations, with an abatement of air transportation-related taxes until the panel made its report. It was not until August 1993 that Liberal Leader Jean Chrétien urged the government to appoint a special airline troubleshooter as a "facilitator" in solving the dispute.

The New Democratic Party recommended that if the National Transportation Agency ruled against the CAIL-AMR deal, the federal government should invest what AMR would have. The NDP said that the $246 million involved would be less than the $340 million the government invested in the Hibernia oil project. In return, the NDP advocated that the government should get the same number of seats – two – that AMR would have had on Canadian Airlines' board. The NDP said it was not proposing permanent government ownership of Canadian and that Canadian should be required to buy back the government's shares at a set value over a period of time.

However, in these days of government pledges of spending cutbacks, this idea would have had trouble gaining widespread support. Also, Canadian Airlines might not have wanted government representatives on its board.

Sidney Fattedad, the man who almost overnight put together the employee investment plan to help save PWA, had taken early retirement a few months before at the age of forty-eight from his position as CAIL's vice-president, Western region. A native of Vancouver, he had decided to move there from Calgary because he believed Vancouver's educational system would be more suitable for his son who has Down's Syndrome. In his view, Vancouver was better at integrating handicapped children into the school system. On returning to Vancouver, Fattedad went into the business of financing home construction.

CAIL employees preferred an alliance with AMR because fewer jobs would be lost – about 1,300 – than under an Air Canada/Canadian merger – as many as 10,000. Fattedad agreed to help on an unpaid basis, charging the unions only for related long-distance telephone calls and travel expenses. He did all the work for them from his home office.

Fattedad said that before proceeding he wanted the official backing of at least one of Canadian's seven unions. The pilots, who were leading many of the demonstrations against the Air Canada deal, agreed to be the initial sponsor. Just a few days later, on the August Civic Holiday weekend,

Fattedad finished drawing up the employee investment plan. In addition to the employee equity infusion, the plan called for the unions to extend their collective agreements until December 31, 1995 and to accept wage increases tied to productivity gains.

Upon the pilots approving his plan, Fattedad presented it to the other unions on August 10. Six of the seven accepted it and formed a representative umbrella organization, the Council of Canadian Airlines Employees, for the express purpose of promoting the plan.

The only union that did not join was the Canadian Auto Workers which has represented reservation agents at Canadian since 1990 and those at Air Canada and PWA since 1985. CAW president Buzz Hargrove says the CAW urged its employees to stay out of the Council because the plan "involved major concessions and the CAW didn't feel they were the solution to Canadian's problems." As a result of this refusal, Hargrove says Rhys Eyton would not bargain with the CAW for months, nor respond to its telephone calls and faxes in the hope that the CAW would change its mind in order to gain his attention.

The CAW wanted to make certain that AMR would not transfer the nine hundred reservation agent jobs at Canadian to its U.S. operations as part of Canadian's switch to its Sabre reservations system. Ultimately, it was agreed that such a transfer would not occur before 1995, the year that the CAW's current contract expires. In return, the CAW extended its collective agreement until December 31, 1995 and accepted the provision tying wages to productivity increases. It also agreed to a reduction in Canadian reservation offices from seven to three. However, the CAW did not join the Council of Canadian Airlines Employees. Fattedad acted as a broker between Canadian and the CAW. His winning argument was "We need to show the politicians that we are united."

Fattedad says his most difficult task was winning the trust of the unions and management. "At first, the union leaders suspected I was acting on behalf of management," he says. "For their part, management wondered if I was a turncoat. On the whole there wasn't a warm embrace by senior management of what I was doing even though the employees were helping save the company." However, he did receive strong support from a very important source – Rhys Eyton – as well as from PWA's board. When the National Transportation Agency ruled on May 27, 1993 in favour of the AMR investment in Canadian, it was exactly ten months from the date Fattedad began working on the employee investment plan, and he celebrated by going to his first party in all that time.

Fattedad says that as a director of PWA he has two goals – a healthy balance sheet and greater management-union cooperation. "PWA did most things right, but I am anti-going into debt, anti-expansion at any price, and anti-market share wars that are too strong and too deep," he says in a remark in which the criticism of the last part virtually nullifies the praise at the beginning. Noting that he was "impressed by the tremendous amount of genuine goodwill on the part of union leaders toward the company," Fattedad says he will urge more open discussion and joint analysis of strategies.

Besides coming to PWA's rescue financially, the employees' loyalty helped restore harmony to PWA's board of directors. The atmosphere among them had become "pretty testy in the summer of 1992 when we were under a lot of pressure, struggling to decide between the Air Canada and AMR proposals," recalls Murray Sigler, a director at the time as well as president of Canadian Regional Airlines. All the directors were under tremendous strain; one was near tears when he told British Columbia officials about PWA's plight and his own possible bankruptcy under potential directors' liability claims. Tension at the board peaked when some directors, without the consent of the rest, urged the federal government to help PWA reach a merger with Air Canada. Their pleas resulted in the government's July 27 ultimatum that PWA resume negotiations with its rival in order to obtain financial assistance. The other board members were infuriated at the government's intervention.

But the employees' willingness to invest millions of dollars in PWA, provided that instead it pursued the AMR alliance, so impressed everyone on the board that it became totally unified in favour of this deal. The unanimity was reinforced by Air Canada's cancelling a merger offer that fall shortly after making it. Subsequently, all the directors lobbied their contacts in the financial community to line up support for PWA's restructuring among its lenders. Also, being from all parts of Canada, they sought to build up public backing across the country for PWA's survival.

The on-again, off-again merger proposals between Air Canada and PWA and how they threatened not just PWA's existence but also competition in Canada's airline industry are described in the next chapter. The many aspects of the AMR-CAIL deal including Air Canada's manoeuvres to block CAIL's withdrawal from Gemini and Air Canada's investment in Continental are also covered.

CHAPTER SIX

Troubled Skies (1990 – 1994, Part II)

From 1991 through 1993, Air Canada proposed three types of associations with PWA: a full merger; a partial merger of their international operations; or the purchase of Canadian Airlines' international routes. Air Canada's chairman Hollis Harris said a merger would produce "substantial advantages including the creation of a strong Canadian-owned airline industry that can compete effectively in the global aviation market; medium and long-term employment growth; and a more rational domestic route and fare structure." Opponents maintained that instead there would be substantial disadvantages. Their list included the elimination of up to 10,000 jobs; one of the highest debt loads among the world's largest airlines; duplication of facilities; too many planes; lack of fleet similarity; and the hostility between the two companies.

Although its proposals took various forms, Air Canada's principal objective was to acquire CAIL's lucrative international routes. Air Canada's and CAIL's international revenues are about equal. CAIL made half its revenue internationally – $1.4 billion in 1992; and Air Canada, 45 percent – $1.6 billion. But it has been predicted that air travel to the Asia Pacific region where Canadian flies will grow faster in the coming years than in Europe and North America where Air Canada flies.

The two airlines overlap in only seven foreign destinations – London, Manchester, Paris and Frankfurt in Europe, and San Francisco, Los Angeles and Honolulu in the United States. However, the points of origin in Canada are not entirely identical. For example, CAIL flies from Vancouver to San Francisco whereas Air Canada does not; by contrast, Air Canada flies nonstop from Toronto to San Francisco, whereas a change to a connecting flight is necessary via CAIL.

Air Canada might not have approached PWA if it had not passed up the opportunity to get the Sydney, Australia and Tokyo routes in the late 1940s. When Air Canada rejected them, the routes went to Canadian

Pacific Airlines which PWA acquired in 1987. So eager was Air Canada to obtain CAIL's international routes that its representative on Gemini's board suggested a major concession in order to obtain them. "If we can gain strategic advantage by trading international route rights for a smooth exit from Gemini, it is certainly worth pursuing," he wrote in an internal memo in November 1992. But, his advice was not followed.

Hollis Harris depicted the offer to purchase CAIL's international routes as "a workable solution that will allow Canadian to restructure into a powerful domestic carrier while also creating a globally competitive Canadian flag carrier." He strongly denied PWA chairman Rhys Eyton's charge that the offer was a "diabolical plot to kill Canadian." Harris responded: "Some have criticized Air Canada as intransigent and inflexible, interested only in destroying PWA and reaping the spoils of a monopoly. This is patently untrue. Instead, we are showing that bankruptcy is not the only alternative to Canadian's deal with AMR."

However, PWA's existence was threatened first by the merger offers and then by the bid for its international routes. The one time the two airlines got as far as a pre-merger agreement, in October 1992, Air Canada would have owned 60 percent of the new company, and PWA 40 percent. But Air Canada withdrew the following month, saying the merger would not produce a "viable" airline. Had the deal gone ahead, it would have been more a takeover by Air Canada than a merger. There would have been a certain irony to a takeover because PWA itself was the product of many takeovers of other airlines, starting in its earliest days and culminating in the acquisition of CP Air in 1987 and Wardair in 1989.

If PWA had accepted the August 1993 $1 billion offer for its international routes, the outcome for it would have been an unhappy one. In the first place, it would have received only $200 million in cash; the rest of the offer would have entailed Air Canada's assuming $800 million worth of debt and lease obligations on eight Canadian Airlines' planes. In addition, PWA would have been thrust back to its domestic-only status before acquiring CP Air.

What a merged Air-Canada Canadian Airlines would have been called was never specified. Some speculated it would be Air Canadian; analysts jokingly named it Mapleflot after Aeroflot, the flag carrier of the former Soviet Union.

In terms of passenger traffic, Air Canada and CAIL were very close. In 1992, Air Canada's passenger revenue was $2.8 billion and CAIL'S, $2.3 billion. Air Canada flew 14.4 billion revenue passenger miles, and CAIL 13.3 billion. Revenue passenger miles refers to the total number of passengers multiplied by the distance they are carried.

If Air Canada's and PWA's revenue had been consolidated in 1991, the first year a merger was proposed, it would have amounted to $6.4 billion. That would have placed it eleventh among the world's airlines. In actuality, Air Canada ranked nineteenth and PWA twenty-third. But, even combined, they would still have been just about half the size of each of American, United and Delta, the world's top three carriers in terms of revenue.

A merger might have yielded some cost-saving benefits. As a monopoly, the capacity could have been reduced which would have raised profitability. "For example, Air Canada and CAIL could easily have reduced their total of daily westbound flights from Toronto to Vancouver from fifteen to twelve for a 20 percent reduction in capacity," says Jacques Kavafian, airline industry analyst at Lévesque Beaubien Geoffrion. Consequently, fewer planes would have been needed, thus lowering fuel and maintenance expenses, as well as landing fees. Kavafian estimates $600 million would have been saved.

Since "Mapleflot" probably would have retained only about 23,000 employees of the total 33,830, it would also have spent about $600 million less a year on salaries, Kavafian calculates. Because all these measures probably would have improved profits, investor interest might have been regained, making a new share issue possible. Both airlines had exhausted their equity bases as of 1993.

However, the drawbacks far outweighed the potential advantages. With a total debt load of $7.7 billion, "Mapleflot" would have carried the sixth-largest debt load among the world's airlines and, in terms of total debt to revenue, at 120.22 percent, it would have had the dubious distinction of ranking first. (Total debt includes perpetual debt, operating leases and capital leases.) "A debt level greater than revenue is a difficult burden to surmount," says Tony Hine, airline analyst at ScotiaMcLeod. "Even a profitable airline would find it hard to service debt as high as its revenue. That extra $1 billion in debt over revenue could have been backbreaking for the new carrier."

Against this debt load, "Mapleflot" would have started life with a disappearing equity base. Air Canada's equity had shrunk from $1 billion in 1989 to $316 million by the end of 1992 and PWA's from $621.8 million to $25 million. Combined, therefore, they would have had an equity base of only $341 million; this would have been eaten up in 1993 by severance costs for laid-off workers and ongoing losses.

Due to the proposed merged airline's precarious financial outlook, Air Canada estimated it would require $1 to $1.5 billion in financial restructuring in order to have a reasonable chance for profitability. Hollis Harris calculated the money would come from the sale of surplus planes and about eighteen months later a new equity issue for $400 to $500 million, backed by federal government guarantees of about $300 million. However, this was wishful thinking because the government had made it plain it would not provide financial assistance.

Predictions as to how many employees "Mapleflot" would have laid off ranged from 6,000 to 10,000. Based on the higher – and more likely – figure, severance costs alone would have amounted to more than $200 million. With fewer people, "Mapleflot" would have required less space. In view of the limited demand for commercial real estate, "Mapleflot" would have been unable to break leases. Jacques Kavafian predicted it would have 2.2 million square feet of excess space for which it might have to pay up to $40 million annually.

"Mapleflot" could have cut occupancy costs by consolidating management at one location, but this would have undoubtedly sparked protests in both Eastern and Western Canada since Air Canada is headquartered in Montreal and CAIL in Calgary. Air Canada promised that each airline would be run independently, with its own head office, but this might have turned out to be temporary, just as PWA's pledge to retain Wardair's separate entity was not kept. As Steven Garmaise, airline analyst at investment dealer First Marathon Securities, said, "This proposal makes political and public relations sense but is an economic idiocy. To be viable and competitive, the proposed company must reduce duplicated facilities and personnel. Fears of bankruptcy should overcome the political fallout of rationalization."

In terms of their plane fleets, there would have been few gains from a merger. At that time, the two airlines had a combined fleet of 190 planes. Kavafian said about twenty-three would have been classified as excess; Garmaise, as many as thirty-five to fifty. Their disposal would have posed a big problem due to the vast glut worldwide of used aircraft. In the case of surplus planes that "Mapleflot" leased, rather than owned, it would have had to pay heavy penalties to break the leases before their expiry dates. Probably more Air Canada than CAIL planes would have been put up for sale because the average age of its fleet was five years older than CAIL's.

Another disadvantage was the lack of fleet commonality. CAIL's planes were primarily Boeing 737s, and Air Canada's, McDonnell Douglas DC-9s. Both had Boeing 767s, but Air Canada's 767s used Pratt & Whitney engines whereas CAIL's 767s were powered by General Electric engines. Although both owned the Airbus 320, these accounted for a small portion of their total fleets.

If instead of a full or partial merger Air Canada had acquired CAIL's international routes, analyst Jacques Kavafian said the reversion to domestic-only status would have benefited PWA. "When it was a domestic airline before 1986, it was profitable," he explained. "As a domestic-only carrier, it could downsize and become very profitable. The most profitable U.S. airlines are domestic-only ones. Of course, it would be a touchy issue to shrink PWA into a domestic carrier because ego would be involved."

However, PWA officials maintained it was far more than a matter of ego; they said PWA's survival was threatened. According to them, when faced with a choice between flying on a solely domestic carrier and one with both domestic and international routes, passengers would choose the latter in order to take advantage of frequent-flier programs and the convenience of a fuller route network. Moreover, Canadian would lose the interconnecting traffic between its international and domestic routes which accounts for one-fifth of its domestic revenue.

Air Canada and PWA also clashed over the potential impact on jobs. Air Canada offered to hire about two thousand CAIL employees. PWA maintained it would mean as many as eight thousand of CAIL's 14,600 employees likely losing their jobs, based on its argument that CAIL would be severely hurt domestically. In that PWA's share and debenture holders were due to vote a week later on PWA's restructuring plan, chairman Rhys Eyton and airline analysts believed Air Canada was attempting to get the voters to accept its offer rather than approve the plan. However, the share and debenture holders stood by PWA, approving the restructuring plan by an overwhelming vote of close to 97 percent.

Considering the years of ill-will between the two airlines, the chances of a harmonious merger were virtually nil. Airline analysts describe their feud as the most intense in the entire industry worldwide, which is saying a lot. "Air Canada's goal – a unique one – has always been to put other Canadian airlines out of business," says Jacques Kavafian. "It has always wanted access to Asia and believed the best way to obtain it was to get the other guy on his knees."

The recent war of words between Air Canada and PWA has often been venomous. In response to Hollis Harris's bid for CAIL's international routes, Eyton snapped: "I've had enough of the arrogance of a former Crown corporation and of the gunslinger from Georgia to tell us how to organize our Canadian airline structure." Executives at both companies seem to have difficulty in saying the other's name. Air Canada's managers call their firm "the red team" and CAIL "the blue team," a reference to the colours on the exterior of their planes. Some at Air Canada mispronounce CRAL, the acronym for Canadian Regional Airlines, as CRAWL.

Moreover, the feud had existed for decades, from the battle over Air Canada's monopoly to the competition for international routes. Also, for many years they were the antithesis of each other – Air Canada was government-owned and PWA was a private enterprise except for the nine years the Alberta government owned it.

While lambasting one another during the crisis, senior executives at the two airlines were charming to the media, their chief conduit to the public. They apologized profusely to me if they had to change interview appointment times, explaining they were a "bit busy." The crisis forced them to work longer than the average eight-hour work day, but they understated the pressure as "business as usual, with an edge to it," as Peter Wallis of CAIL put it. Once, however, he did express himself more colourfully: "We're up to our rear end in alligators!"

PWA was not alone in its concern over a merger. Travel agents and consumers were also worried. Commissions from the airlines for ticket sales constitute a major portion of travel companies' revenues. In 1986, before PWA acquired CP Air and Wardair, the commissions for travel within Canada were 10 percent from Wardair, 9.25 percent from CP Air, 9 percent from PWA, and 8.25 percent from Air Canada. Under the Air Canada–PWA duopoly, they were the lowest rate, the 8.25 percent Air Canada had paid previously. Travel agents were concerned that if Canada were to have a single national airline, their commissions would drop further. Under such circumstances, many feared their businesses would fail.

Consumers were apprehensive they would be adversely affected by a monopoly since without competition air fares would undoubtedly spiral and the number of destinations flown within Canada shrink. Canadian Airlines and its regional affiliates fly to more places – 108 – in Canada than Air Canada and its regional connectors – 67. The likelihood of a new competitor taking on "Mapleflot" was slim at best. The charter airlines offer far less frequent service and Nationair, the largest charter operator, went out of business in 1993.

A new scheduled airline likely would not have lasted long because it would have lacked many or all of the elements necessary for success: the money to buy sufficient planes; well-located airport facilities; a frequent-flier program; feeder traffic from a regional network and from international airlines; and priority listing on a computerized reservations system.

The federal government might have said that the proposed "open skies" agreement with the United States would inject competition because U.S. airlines would be allowed to fly from place to place within Canada. But although there have been years of talks about "open skies," it could take as long as ten years for a deal to be reached according to airline analysts. Nonetheless, even if "open skies" did exist, the U.S. airlines have never expressed interest in flying within Canada. "Mapleflot" would have faced competition on international flights from foreign carriers, just as Air Canada and CAIL do now. But since these carriers only fly to and from major Canadian cities, much of Canada would not have benefited.

When their October 8, 1992 pre-merger agreement was terminated on November 3 by Air Canada, PWA pursued its "Project Iceberg" talks with AMR. On December 29 they signed a "strategic alliance" under which AMR would invest $246 million in Canadian Airlines in return for a one-third equity and one-fourth voting interest and conditional on Canadian's transferring to AMR's Sabre system. The original deadline was September 30, 1993, but it was extended to the end of the year because of PWA's problems in extricating itself from Gemini.

In the intervening months between the December 29 signing and the start of the National Transportation Agency hearings March 22, 1993 on whether to allow AMR's investment, an AMR subsidiary won against Air Canada in a court case, adding to the ill-will between the two airlines. In 1986, AMR had bought Ticketnet Corporation, then a two-year-old Ottawa-based company that had developed a computerized box office booking system in which tickets for theatre performances and sports events in one part of a country could be booked from another. Air Canada was helping Ticketnet in its software development because it believed the concept was applicable to the airline industry as well, such as for low-cost express ticketing, without name, address, or refunds. There was nothing in their agreement prohibiting Ticketnet from forming a relationship with other airlines.

The dispute between Ticketnet and Air Canada arose four months before AMR acquired Ticketnet; it was caused mainly by clashing corporate cultures. As a small young company, Ticketnet needed to put its product on the market quickly to generate revenue, but Air Canada, with its huge bureaucracy, moved slowly. The clash resulted in Air Canada's breaking its software agreement with Ticketnet for which Ticketnet sued for breach of contract.

Not only did Ticketnet win the case, it was awarded close to $18 million in damages by Justice James Farley of the Ontario Court of Justice's General Division. AMR derived pleasure from both its subsidiary's victory and the harsh criticism Justice Farley heaped upon Air Canada as "reprehensible," with an "almost arrogant big company attitude." In a vivid analogy, he also said, "One should not impose a legal burden on one party to be the faithful and obedient dog continuing to lick the other party's hand when in effect that other party has been continually swatting it with a newspaper."

Cross-border ownership in the airline industry was common well before AMR and PWA began talking about an AMR investment in CAIL. Unlike marketing agreements that are less stable because they can easily be cancelled, an equity alliance enables the participants to retain their separate identities while at the same time operating aggressive shared marketing programs. Either just one carrier buys into the other, as in the case of AMR and CAIL, or each buys a piece of the other. There were close to twenty such alliances by airlines around the world before the AMR-CAIL negotiations started.

Strategic alliances are intended as a win-win arrangement for both participants and that is how Canadian Airlines International and AMR perceived their deal. PWA had insisted that AMR invest in CAIL in return for CAIL's subscribing to AMR's computerized management services programs covering accounting, data processing and operations planning. Not only did these programs contain advanced technology that CAIL could not have afforded to develop itself, CAIL expected they also would enable it to reduce its costs by $30 million annually, thereby significantly strengthening its balance sheet. In addition CAIL anticipated annual gains of $27 million in revenue from American's feeding traffic to it, a link that would be boosted by reciprocal privileges regarding frequent-flier programs.

For its part, AMR expected that CAIL would pay it $100 to $115 million annually for these services, so that AMR would recoup its $246-million investment in little more than the first two years. All told, American would make $2 billion during the contract's twenty-year life. Even if CAIL is unprofitable, it must pay AMR. The twenty-year duration of the contract is the typical length of AMR's services contracts. "For an airline the size of American, a $246-million investment is a small amount of money, comparable to feeding the goose that lays the golden eggs," says Ted Larkin of Bunting Warburg. "If the goose isn't fed, it will die."

Although AMR lost money and laid off employees in 1992, so did Air Canada, and its far heavier losses did not prevent it from making offers to PWA for a full or partial merger or its international routes. Moreover, AMR had been profitable in 1990 and 1991, whereas Air Canada had not been.

Equally important as the $2 billion American would make, the scope of the contract would provide a showcase to which AMR could point in its sales pitch to other companies. AMR has decided to reduce the size of its airline operations which accounted for its losses in 1992 and focus on its fast-growing, profitable contract services businesses. Lufthansa uses AMR technology to track flight operations and check in passengers and two U.S. airlines, Southwest and Alaska, use AMR's Sabre system to handle reservations made with their airlines. But the CAIL deal is the first to cover so many aspects of running an airline.

"By far the most important part of the transaction from AMR's perspective is the services agreement," AMR executive vice-president Donald Carty said. AMR's contract services division is one of his responsibilities. "Our focus in the next decade will be on growing this information side of our business. We would like to provide this package of services to a number of other airlines around the world. That's why the Canadian package is strategic for us. It's an idealized model."

The National Transportation Agency approved AMR's investment in CAIL on May 27. Within days, on June 2, Air Canada appealed to the federal Cabinet to overrule the NTA. Under the terms of the National Transportation Act, the Cabinet had thirty days from the date of the decision in which to take action. On June 23, it said it would not overturn the decision.

Air Canada officials appeared surprised and angry at the NTA's decision. Their reaction partly arose from a newspaper reporter with excellent sources in the NTA having written some days earlier that it would rule against the AMR investment. In addition, Air Canada executives believed that precedent was against CAIL based on two previous cases they regarded as similar.

In 1989, the NTA cancelled the licence of Minerve Canada, a charter airline formed two years earlier, on the grounds that its financial and operating relationship with Minerve S.A., a French company, gave Minerve S.A. "control in fact." Therefore, the NTA concluded Minerve Canada lacked sufficient Canadian content to continue to have its licence. The second example Air Canada cited was the 1991 application of two U.S. partners to invest in Worldways Canada, a large charter operator that had sought the investment after its credit was cut off. The NTA rejected the application on the grounds of insufficient Canadian content. Subsequently, Worldways went out of business.

Air Canada based its opposition to the AMR-CAIL deal on allegations that AMR would have too much control over CAIL, rather than against the 25 percent voting interest it would have because that amount is allowable under the National Transportation Act. Moreover, Air Canada itself had expressed support for raising the foreign voting control ceiling to 49 percent, an expansion also advocated by two federal government studies released while the AMR-CAIL deal was under discussion. Both the Report of the Royal Commission on National Passenger Transportation and the National Transportation Act Review Commission said that foreign ownership would be "pro-competitive" because it would provide existing and potential Canadian airlines with greater access to capital.

Canadian and AMR officials insisted that AMR did not want, nor would it gain, control over Canadian. However, the deal did grant it considerable influence. Although it would only have two of the eight directors on CAIL's board, they would have power of approval over a wide variety of financial items, with an annual approval threshold set for each. These included declaring dividends in excess of $5 million; selling more than $20 million in assets; borrowing or spending more than $30 million; and capital expenditures over $50 million.

That amount is equivalent to the cost of just one large plane. Nevertheless, CAIL officials professed unconcern. They emphasized AMR would have no veto power over Canadian's commitments already made for planes throughout the rest of the 1990s. "It is in AMR's interest for CAIL to have more planes because they would increase our demand for AMR's yield management projections regarding capacity and pricing," explained Peter Wallis. He also pointed out that directors must exercise their powers to a company's benefit. "The more profitable Canadian becomes, the greater the volume it will be able to buy in services from AMR," he continued. "Therefore, it would be in AMR's interest to focus on what would be good for Canadian."

AMR's management services programs would significantly determine how Canadian is run because they cover every aspect of the company from accounting to fares. Also, the initiative of CAIL management might be curbed by reluctance to take the risk of contradicting AMR's computer analysis. AMR is also partly responsible for PWA's planned organizational restructuring whereby the regional airlines and holiday tour companies are to become subsidiaries of CAIL.

The planned shuffle prompted the resignation in June 1993 of Murray Sigler who had developed the regional airline network and served as president of Canadian Regional Airlines from when it was established in 1991. He had hoped it would be spun off as a separate company. When instead it was decided to shift the regionals under CAIL, he decided he "would have less to do" because CRAL's finances and marketing, as well as its strategic and corporate planning, would be integrated with CAIL'S.

He began a consulting firm, operating from an office at Canadian Airlines until the end of October 1993 when he resigned from PWA's board of directors. He says he waited until then because "I did not want to give the impression that I was not supportive of PWA's restructuring plan and management when, in reality, I did support them." Also, he wanted to remain until the restructuring "was pretty much completed." But, as his consulting business grew, he decided to break away completely so as to avoid potential conflicts of interest.

* * *

Whether to support the proposed Air Canada-Canadian merger or the AMR-CAIL deal was a dilemma for the Canadian public because each had advantages and disadvantages. The merit of a single airline was that it would be fully Canadian-owned; the drawback would be that it would create a monopoly. By contrast, AMR's investment in CAIL would preserve competition by ensuring that Canada would still have two airlines, but the price would be loss of part of the ownership to a foreign company.

Opinion among public advocacy groups was divided. The Council of Canadians which endorses a "strong, independent, Canadian-owned economy" advocated the first option. The Consumers' Association of Canada which favours "strong competition" backed the second.

"A Canadian-controlled airline industry is essential to the national and public interest," the Council of Canadians maintained. "The fundamental problem with foreign ownership is that it leads inevitably to key commercial decisions, with important social and economic implications, being made outside Canada. This makes it much more difficult to enforce national standards and regulations regarding labour, service and financial operations. . . . In this case the potential for damage to the national interest is all the greater, given the importance of the airline and related industries to Canada's economic development at the dawn of the twenty-first century."

The Consumers' Association of Canada supported the AMR-CAIL deal because "consumers benefit from a competitive airline industry through access to convenient, affordable service. Our primary concern is not so much who is providing the service but the conditions under which that service is delivered, and we oppose anti-competitive behaviour."

If the AMR-CAIL deal had depended only on the National Transportation Agency's approval, it would have been finalized quickly and smoothly. It was AMR's stipulation that CAIL transfer from Gemini to its Sabre computerized reservations system that made the outcome uncertain. The suspense was caused by the diametrically opposed opinions of the forums where the Gemini issue was contested. The Ontario Court of Justice's General Division and the Ontario Court of Appeal ruled against PWA (the parent of CAIL which used the system), saying CAIL could not switch. Although the quasi-judicial federal Competition Tribunal leaned toward PWA, it was reluctant to get involved until forced to and its hesitation caused the issue to drag on for months.

Thanks to the speed of computerized systems, airline reservations today can be made in a few minutes' time. But, in the early days of airplane travel, no such technology existed. At first reservations were made by radio operators, a slow procedure taking as long as twenty-four hours. During World War II the airlines began using teletype, but confirmations were no faster. Then, in the 1950s, Air Canada had the foresight to be one of the world's first airlines to develop a computerized reservations system. Called "Reservec" (for reservations electronically controlled), it dominated Canada's airline industry for thirty years because no other airline developed a rival system. Although Reservec did include information on competitors' flights and fares, their schedules were listed lower. Since, in Canada, travel agents sell 70 percent of airline tickets and half their sales come from the first line displayed on the computer screen, Air Canada had a big advantage over its competitors, principally CP Air which flew many of the same routes. Moreover, CP Air had to pay Air Canada a fee for its tickets sold through Reservec.

But it was not until 1984 that CP Air launched its own system, calling it "Pegasus" after the winged horse in Greek mythology. However, due to Air Canada's having already signed up most of Canada's travel agents to Reservec and few travel agents being able to afford both systems, Pegasus only achieved a 5 percent market share. Moreover, CP Air still had to pay Air Canada a fee for every CP Air ticket sold on Reservec, whereas Air Canada refused to do the reverse.

Its challenge having failed, CP Air approached Air Canada about merging their systems. When Air Canada declined, CP Air began to negotiate with American Airlines to use American's Sabre system, the world's leading airline reservation system, as a replacement for Pegasus, an early version of the proposed transfer of Canadian Airlines to Sabre from Gemini.

CP Air's threat to join Sabre forced Air Canada to change its mind about a joint system. But by the time an agreement was reached, CP Air had been purchased by Pacific Western Airlines and PWA's and CP Air's operations had been merged under the name Canadian Airlines International (CAIL). Therefore, it was PWA that completed the negotiations. On July 1, 1987, Air Canada and PWA merged their systems under the name The Gemini Group Automated Distribution Systems. Each owned 50 percent, even though Air Canada put in more money ($89 million) than PWA ($39 million). It was to be an eighty-year partnership lasting until December 31, 2067.

In that Gemini had a near monopoly with a 90 percent market share, Wardair and the Consumers' Association of Canada asked the federal government's Competition Tribunal to dissolve it on the grounds that it was anti-competitive. In April 1989, after Air Canada and PWA promised timely and complete information would be provided on competitors' schedules, the Competition Tribunal approved their formation of Gemini.

At the beginning of July 1989, Gemini admitted a new partner – Covia, a computerized reservations system 50 percent-owned by United Airlines and the other half by a number of U.S. and European airlines. Covia invested $35 million in Gemini and Gemini adopted Covia's state-of-the-art technology. Ownership of Gemini became divided four ways – 33 percent each by Air Canada, PWA and Covia and the remaining one percent by Gemini itself.

Gemini makes annual revenue of $150 million and employs seven hundred people, based primarily in Winnipeg. About 20 to 23 percent of Gemini's revenue came from CAIL and the rest from Air Canada, sixteen local airlines, Via Rail, the Department of National Defence, and Marine Atlantic, a federal water transportation agency. Until its 1993 demise, Nationair, Canada's largest charter airline and the third-biggest after Air Canada and CAIL, was a client, too.

From its outset, Gemini has had two functions. One is the provision of information and booking services to travel agents for making reservations and issuing tickets. The other role is the management – called "hosting" – of the internal reservations systems used by the airlines for seat inventory. Hosting of Pegasus, CAIL'S internal reservation system, is to move to Sabre as part of the arrangement whereby American would give CAIL access to its computer-based information and management support systems on all aspects of running an airline more profitably. Because data from these systems and Sabre are integrated, CAIL would have to transfer to Sabre.

It is not unusual for companies to withdraw from business arrangements if they believe it is in their best interest to do so. For example, Air Canada itself had done this to Ticketnet. Another example is Gulf Canada Resources' 1992 pull-out from the Hibernia project because it believed it was too heavy a financial burden; until a replacement was found, Hibernia's future was in jeopardy. Moreover, The Limited Partnerships Act allows dissolution of partnerships under a wide variety of circumstances.

But in the case of Gemini, there were only two ways a partner could withdraw. Provided the other partners agreed, Air Canada or PWA could terminate their participation in 1999, after giving two years' notice. This date was too far in the future for PWA because AMR had stipulated that CAIL must transfer to Sabre by the end of 1993. The alternative way the contract could be broken was if Gemini were to become insolvent. It is astounding that all the high-priced legal talent representing both airlines boxed them into just these two circumstances for breaking the contract; they should have allowed for the unexpected.

That PWA regretted not having done better is apparent from a comment made in a speech October 25, 1993 to the Calgary Chamber of Commerce by Murray Sigler, then a PWA board member as well as PWA's nominee to Gemini's board since June 1993. Talking about the lessons that he had learned from PWA's "successes and disappointments" throughout his sixteen years at the company, he said: "Always negotiate an out for the unmentionable, unforeseeable events that can happen down the road. So many times, you'll end up wanting to dispose of what you've bought, or wanting to end a partnership once thought made in Heaven. Avoid the acrimony and litigation by working it out upfront."

Although there was no contractual provision, a third possible escape route for PWA was to try to buy its way out, a common procedure. PWA offered $51 million in compensation – its Gemini shares which it valued at $30 million and the rest in cash – and also expressed a willingness to negotiate further. But Gemini rejected the offer, saying "It doesn't come close to the substantial losses Gemini would suffer if Canadian withdrew." Based on the approximately $30 to $34.5 million CAIL paid Gemini annually, the offer was much less than what Gemini anticipated making by 1999, the earliest year for PWA to contractually withdraw.

In view of Gemini's rejection of compensation and of AMR's year-end 1993 deadline, the only withdrawal option left for PWA under the terms of the Gemini contract was to have Gemini declared insolvent. Its attempt to do so was one of several strange features of the Gemini dispute. While alleging that Gemini was insolvent, PWA itself was trying to avoid liquidation. On November 29, 1992, PWA suspended payments to its creditors for five months. Also, each side contradicted itself. PWA maintained Gemini was insolvent, at the same time it insisted Gemini would do fine without PWA's business. Gemini said it was solvent but would be irreparably damaged if PWA withdrew.

In addition, the conflict pitted a 100 percent foreign-owned system – Sabre – against a 33 percent foreign-owned one – Gemini. Covia, the foreign partner, processed Gemini transactions at its Denver operations and then routed them back to Gemini in Canada. A further curious aspect was that PWA's representatives on Gemini were accused of fiduciary irresponsibility while, at the same time, PWA maintained "directors must exercise their powers to a company's benefit" regarding the vetos AMR would have over CAIL.

PWA's efforts to extricate itself from Gemini began on August 31, 1992 when it asked the Queen's Bench Division of the Alberta Supreme Court to declare Gemini insolvent. The next day, at a Gemini board meeting, PWA's representative tabled a motion calling for Gemini to be dissolved and a receiver appointed. The other board members angrily refused. The following day, Air Canada made its third merger proposal to PWA in which Air Canada would have 60 percent, and PWA 40 percent.

The Gemini situation simmered until November when events piled up on one another. On November 3, Air Canada terminated the pre-merger agreement. On November 5, Howard Wetston, then head of the federal government's Bureau of Competition Policy, recommended that the Competition Tribunal enable PWA to extricate itself from Gemini through rescinding or changing the Tribunal's April 1989 consent order to Gemini's formation. Wetston did so because he believed a merger would be anti-competitive. "If an Air Canada-PWA merger were to take place, or if PWA were to cease operations, the result would be a monopoly in most domestic airline markets in Canada," he said in explaining his intervention. On November 10, the Queen's Bench Division of the Alberta Supreme Court "stayed" proceedings in the insolvency case filed August 31 by PWA. On November 12, Gemini filed a $1-billion lawsuit against PWA claiming breach of fiduciary duties as well as a $500-million lawsuit against both PWA and AMR claiming unlawful interference in Gemini's economic interests. The breach of fiduciary duties charge pertained to PWA's not notifying the Gemini partners that the deal with AMR would require CAIL to withdraw from Gemini. On December 2, Covia launched a $1.2-billion lawsuit against PWA for breach of fiduciary duties.

There was a lapse in the Gemini warfare until April 2, 1993 when the Ontario Court of Justice's General Division, to which the Queen's Bench Division of the Alberta Supreme Court had transferred the case, rejected PWA's lawsuit that Gemini be declared insolvent. Instead, Justice Frank Callaghan said Gemini not only had "been built exactly as planned" but had also performed better than expected financially. Instead of projected losses of $14.5 million in 1991, $18.5 million in 1992, and $1.9 million in 1993, Gemini had 1991 losses of $12.1 million, almost broke even in 1992, and expected to be profitable in 1993. Moreover, its losses were largely due to a one-time event – its $45 million conversion to the Covia technology which was completed in July 1992.

Twenty days later on April 22, the Competition Tribunal said it supported PWA's argument that Gemini would survive without Canadian but that Canadian would "likely fail" if it could not complete its deal with AMR. However, the Competition Tribunal ruled that it lacked the authority to release PWA from Gemini, although one of the three members on the Tribunal maintained it did have the power. But the Tribunal did say that if the Federal Court of Appeal were to decide that the Tribunal had jurisdiction, it would rule in favour of PWA. More time elapsed. Then, on July 30, the Federal Court of Appeal ruled the Tribunal did have authority. That decision buoyed PWA, but on August 11, it suffered a setback when the Ontario Court of Appeal upheld the April 2 decision of the Ontario Court of Justice's General Division.

The Tribunal did not resume its Gemini hearing until November 15 – a lapse of three-and-a-half months after the Federal Court of Appeal's ruling regarding its jurisdiction. On the fourth day of the week-long hearing, a seemingly fresh crisis arose for PWA when AMR's American Airlines subsidiary was virtually shut down by a flight attendants' strike during the U.S. Thanksgiving holiday season, the most lucrative period of the year for airlines in the U.S.

The strike was ended after five days when President Bill Clinton got the strikers and management to agree to binding arbitration. The strike cost American an estimated $10 million a day according to management, $25 million according to the attendants. Nevertheless, both AMR and CAIL officials said the AMR-CAIL deal would proceed, pointing out that it was with AMR, American's parent, rather than American itself.

American's strike ended November 22. Two days later, a week ahead of when its decision was expected, the Competition Tribunal ruled for CAIL's release from its "hosting" contract with Gemini. The Tribunal gave two weeks, until December 8, for PWA-Canadian to reach a negotiated settlement with the other Gemini partners. On December 8, the Tribunal extended the deadline to December 20.

Otherwise, the Tribunal said it would dissolve Gemini a year later in November 1994 by which time CAIL estimated it would have completed its move to Sabre, including the transfer of cabling from ticket offices and the training of travel agents on Sabre's system. For a while afterward, there was the slim possibility that this ruling would prove to be the turning point in the airline crisis, as it forced Air Canada and PWA to accept federal government mediation of their conflict. But the talks failed to reach a compromise.

Throughout the Gemini court cases and Tribunal hearings, the central issue was survival – of CAIL, Gemini, and competition, and hence a choice for consumers. CAIL maintained it would die if not allowed to transfer to Sabre and thereby receive AMR's $246-million investment. Also, its dying would cause extensive shrinkage in competition in Canada's airline industry. Gemini countered that it would die if CAIL were released or, at the very least, it would lose its competitive edge as a result of no longer receiving income from CAIL that it could apply towards maintaining and improving service. Therefore, so many of its customers might switch to Sabre that Sabre would become a monopoly compared to Gemini's existing 65 percent market share and Sabre's 35 percent.

The Competition Tribunal concluded that its duty was "to prevent a lessening of airline competition. Our primary concern must be the protection of the public interest in competition and not the preservation of private contractual settlements." In so doing, it accepted PWA's position. "Without an exit of its hosting from Gemini, Canadian will probably fail, but with an exit, Canadian will probably recover its financial stability," it said.

Because Canadian accounted for only about one-fifth of Gemini's revenue, in theory Gemini should have been able to survive without CAIL's hosting business. Also, Gemini could have continued its other function of supplying travel agents with information on CAIL schedules, fares and seat availability. The Tribunal encouraged the reformulation of Gemini by saying it, Air Canada or Covia could "operate or continue" in the computerized reservations business before or after the dissolution of the Gemini partnership. Gemini's technology could also be used to transmit information about far more than travel; for example, entertainment, financial services and health care.

Even though both Air Canada and Covia had charged that CAIL was thinking only of itself at the expense of Gemini, they proved to be no different. Both told the Tribunal that if CAIL was allowed to withdraw, they would not be prepared to continue as partners in Gemini and would want it dissolved. Air Canada saw no point in continuing since it would be the only "hosted" partner. Covia, of which United Airlines is the largest shareholder, regarded a dissolution as an opportunity to obtain Gemini's customer base and become a direct competitor in Canada to Sabre.

In February 1994, Air Canada announced it would create a new company – Galileo Canada – that will use the Apollo software of Galileo International in which Air Canada and United Airlines are shareholders. Thus, Canada's two major airlines will use foreign technology – typical in the industry. Galileo International, for example, is owned by eleven airlines, including many in Europe, and no objections have been made to its multi-nationalism.

Gemini could also have survived, despite CAIL's departure, if its other customers remained loyal. Significantly, the chief one – government-owned VIA Rail – did not participate in the Tribunal's decisive November 1993 hearing. As the Tribunal noted, these other clients could turn to alternate "hosting" companies.

The Tribunal's conclusion that CAIL's survival depended on its meeting AMR's stipulation that it leave Gemini for Sabre was not shared by the Ontario Court of Justice's General Division or by the Ontario Court of Appeal, with the exception of one judge. Justice Frank Callaghan of the former court maintained that PWA and Air Canada were "sophisticated commercial entities that entered into the Gemini Partnership with their corporate eyes open."

The dissenter at the Ontario Court of Appeal was Justice Charles Dubin. He said CAIL should be allowed to quit Gemini under Section 35 of The Limited Partnerships Act which permits dissolution of partnerships "when circumstances arise that in the opinion of the Court render it just and equitable." Dubin maintained the "likelihood that Canadian would not survive if PWA is forced to remain in the Gemini Partnership is an important relevant factor. The failure of Canadian would not only eliminate an important aspect of competition in the airline industry, but would have a serious impact on thousands of employees and many others."

However, the other two Court of Appeal judges disagreed that PWA's survival depended solely on Gemini's dissolution. They pointed out that the CAIL-AMR deal also relied on other factors. These included the acceptance of PWA's debt restructuring proposal by its creditors; the approval of AMR's investment in CAIL by the National Transportation Agency; and the necessity of PWA's avoiding insolvency or bankruptcy proceedings, as well as large damage claims in the Gemini cases.

Both courts found PWA guilty of fiduciary irresponsibility. Justice Callaghan cited a letter CAIL's president, Kevin Jenkins, wrote to Gemini's president, Paul Nelson, on April 9, 1992, six days after Gemini warned that it would sue CAIL for breach of contract if Gemini transferred to Sabre. "Our discussions with American are proceeding on the basis that we will comply with our contractual obligations regarding Gemini," Jenkins said.

Callaghan concluded: "There is no evidence that PWA ever attempted to approach its partners in a bona fide manner. It is clear that PWA's strategy throughout its negotiations with AMR was to withhold full disclosure and retain flexibility for one purpose only, to implement Project Iceberg."

But the Ontario Court of Appeal's Justice Dubin dissented. He said: "I do not agree there was a duty to disclose the condition of the proposed transaction that Canadian's hosting be removed from Gemini. The hosting provision was an integral part of negotiations towards the tentative agreement and could not be isolated. Thus, in my opinion, it would have been impossible to disclose discussions about the hosting provision without disclosing the transaction which was being negotiated and which affected Canadian's survival as a competitor of Air Canada."

Besides the tangled contractual issues between Gemini and PWA, the court cases highlighted Air Canada's desire that CAIL be unable to leave Gemini because that would shatter the deal with AMR, mortally wounding CAIL. But the judges disagreed as to whether Air Canada was a deliberate spoiler. Justice Callaghan said he was "satisfied" that Air Canada's related memoranda "do not establish a corporate strategy of making Gemini the battleground in Air Canada's struggle to gain a competitive advantage in the airline industry." Justice Dubin disagreed, saying: "The only inference I can draw from the Air Canada memoranda is that, for understandable reasons from its point of view, Air Canada was using the Gemini Partnership to thwart the agreement between PWA and AMR."

Readers, judge for yourselves. In February 1991, Air Canada's then executive vice-president of corporate strategy, who was also a Gemini director, wrote that Air Canada's strategy regarding Gemini should be to "continue to operate while we sort out our own strategic direction: stymie CAIL." A year later on February 25, 1992, five days after Hollis Harris became Air Canada's president, his executive assistant, R.R. Thomson, advised him: "Don't walk away from the PWA merger because as long as we profess interest, it helps prevent an AMR/PWA deal." Thomson testified during the court case that his note reflected "a view from a different perspective that may not coincide with higher legal advice." In any event, as Justice Callaghan pointed out, this memo did not directly refer to Gemini. Moreover, one month after Thomson's memo, on March 12, PWA and AMR signed a letter of intent, and PWA terminated its merger talks with Air Canada on March 19.

The following month, on April 23, Air Canada's corporate secretary advised Air Canada's strategic issues committee that Air Canada should "continue its strategy of slowing down/denying the AMR deal." A July 1992 memo of unspecified date by the director of pricing and revenue went further: "Although it would appear counterproductive to have a dissatisfied partner in Gemini, Air Canada needs to maintain the existing partnership arrangements for the near future to serve as a deterrent and spoiler for the PWA/AMR negotiations." On November 6, 1992, four days before Justice Callaghan began hearing the insolvency case, Air Canada's senior director of corporate communications used even stronger language: "If our delay action fails, Gemini should adopt a 'scorched earth' policy ensuring that any exit is less than congenial."

* * *

During much of the time the Gemini dispute was raging and Air Canada was deriding CAIL for pursuing an alliance with a foreign airline, Air Canada was preparing to do the very same thing. On August 27, 1992, four days before PWA began its court efforts to extricate itself from Gemini, Air Canada made an offer for part ownership of Continental Airlines, Hollis Harris's former employer. Continental is the fifth-largest U.S. airline and its 1992 revenue was twice that of Air Canada. The deal was completed on April 28, 1993, with Air Canada acquiring 27.2 percent of the common and 23.9 percent of the voting stock. Its associate in the transaction, Air Partners, a Fort Worth, Texas investment group, obtained the same amount of common shares, but 40.9 percent of the voting stock. The United States prohibits foreign interests from owning more than 49 percent of the equity and 25 percent of the voting shares in a U.S. airline.

Air Canada paid just U.S.$85 million, having transferred the bulk of its share of the $450-million purchase price over to General Electric Capital Corporation in the form of bonds backed by Continental assets. Analysts praised the deal as a bargain. They also pointed out that whereas the relatively small sum had given Air Canada a stake in a major U.S. airline, the money would have only served to marginally reduce Air Canada's 1992 long-term debt of $2.5 billion.

The deal enabled Continental to emerge from the bankruptcy protection under which it had been since December 1990. In an unfortunate juxtaposition of events on April 29, the day after the deal was completed, Continental Airlines' employees were cheering their good fortune at the same time Hollis Harris was telling Air Canada's annual meeting that 2,200 Air Canada jobs would be eliminated in 1993 as a cost-saving measure.

Air Canada hoped to create a world-scale airline through a combination of itself, Continental and PWA. In terms of revenue, the combined airline would have been close in size to the Big Three U.S. carriers – American, United and Delta. Their total 1992 revenue would have been U.S.$10.9 billion compared to American Airlines' $13.5 billion. Air Canada's 1992 revenue was equivalent to U.S.$2.9 billion.

The combination would have produced cost-saving synergies in purchasing and the three airlines' routes would have complemented one another. Continental has a strong network across the United States. Both it and CAIL fly across the Pacific, whereas Air Canada did not. All three fly to Europe. In addition, Hollis Harris was very knowledgeable about Continental, having been its president before joining Air Canada.

But the advantages would likely have been outweighed by the weaknesses. As *Business Week* put it: "Air Canada is pursuing an audacious strategy of trying to build a giant from a foundation of three weak airlines." There were many barriers. Each airline had massive debt. The United States' restrictions on foreign ownership would have prevented Air Canada from merging all three. Although Continental was a low-cost carrier, it had the poorest operating yields (average revenue per passenger mile) among the major U.S. airlines because relatively few businesspeople were customers. Business travellers who fly business or first class are the most profitable part of the airline business, but the bulk of Continental's passengers were economy-fare leisure travellers. In addition, Continental had a turbulent history. In just seven years it had been in bankruptcy protection twice and in eleven years had had ten presidents.

Moreover, analysts question whether to do well an airline has to be a global megacarrier, such as Air Canada contemplated. "For some reason, Mr. Harris believes it important for Air Canada to be a megacarrier, even though an airline does not have to be big to be successful," says industry analyst Jacques Kavafian. "Two of the world's most successful airlines – Singapore Airlines and Cathay Pacific – have only forty planes each compared to Air Canada's one hundred and fifteen."

Air Canada had opposed the PWA-AMR deal on the grounds that control of a Canadian airline would be handed over to a foreign airline. Therefore, its investment in Continental put it in the awkward position of having to explain why it was perfectly all right for a Canadian airline to invest in an American one, while terribly objectionable for an American airline to do the reverse. Air Canada executives maintained there was no similarity, but they would have been exactly alike if the U.S. Department of Transportation had not intervened. It forced Air Canada to relinquish the veto power it had obtained over most Continental expenditures, the acquisition or sale of many assets, debt financing, and the purchase or lease of aircraft. But it did allow Air Canada right of approval over any possible bankruptcy filing or liquidation by Continental. However, Continental is in much better shape than when it entered bankruptcy protection in 1990. That year it had debt of U.S.\$4.1 billion. In April 1993, its debt was down to \$1.7 billion.

"The U.S. government made it clear that it would not accept the type of veto rights that AMR insisted on in its CAIL deal," says R.A. (Sandy) Morrison, Air Canada's vice-president of corporate communications, government and industry relations. "The relationship is dramatically different. Air Canada is an investor, unlike AMR which insisted on operational control." AMR and CAIL, however, stressed repeatedly that AMR only wanted a "strategic alliance" with CAIL, not control.

Air Canada anticipated a strong traffic boost from its association with Continental, particularly because Continental is the dominant airline at Newark Airport, one of three key airports in the New York City area. Air Canada and Continental plan to link their systems, primarily at Newark. Continental also has a strong hub in Houston and, shortly after its deal with Continental, Air Canada began a Toronto-Houston service connecting into Continental's flights to and from Mexico and Central America. Morrison says the linkage has increased Continental's revenue by 25 percent and Air Canada's "by about the same amount."

Hollis Harris has predicted that, all told, the deal will generate \$400 million in extra revenue for both airlines. But his prediction depends on finalization of a bilateral air traffic agreement covering more cities between the United States and Canada.

The existing bilateral air treaty was signed twenty years ago, in 1974. It restricted Canada's airlines to scheduled flights to just twenty U.S. cities.

In 1990, the two countries began "open skies" talks with the goal of almost unlimited access for carriers to operate in both countries. Harris forecast that the pact would be signed within a year of the Air Canada-Continental deal. The talks subsequently got bogged down and airline analysts say it could take five to ten years for an agreement to be reached.

Air Canada also expects the deal will create millions of dollars in contract service work for the refurbishing of Continental planes and engines. Continental contracts out much of its maintenance work but hitherto, had not done so to Canada. Shortly after Air Canada invested in it, Continental awarded Air Canada a major aircraft maintenance contract resulting in the saving of 155 jobs at Air Canada's Winnipeg maintenance facilities.

Additionally, although the arrangement with Continental was a twosome rather than a threesome including PWA for which Air Canada had hoped, it fulfilled Air Canada's goal of building a global network due to a development shortly afterward. In July 1993, Continental and Air France formed a commercial alliance to coordinate flight schedules, feed passengers to each other, and honour each other's frequent-flier programs. Air Canada will benefit because it had begun a marketing agreement with Air France in April, the same month its investment in Continental was finalized. Thus, it has commercial ties with both Air France and Continental which, in turn, have similar connections with each other.

The linkage plugs Air Canada into a global network. Combined, Continental, Air France and Air Canada fly to four hundred destinations and have approximately seventy-five million passengers. Through Continental and Air France, Air Canada has access to traffic from Latin America, Asia, Africa and the Middle East, places to which it does not fly.

Air Canada's offer to Continental was made just eight days after it signed a marketing agreement with United Airlines covering coordination of schedules, interconnection of travellers and reciprocal frequent flier privileges. United and Air Canada already were well acquainted through Covia, of which United owns half, being a partner in Gemini. Ultimately, the marketing arrangement could cause a conflict because both United and Continental have hubs at Denver. However, Air Canada does not fly to Denver and its alliance with United concentrates on connections between its flights and United's at United's hubs at Chicago's O'Hare airport and San Francisco's airport, where Continental does not have hubs. Air Canada will not have to make a decision about Denver until the new bilateral agreement is reached between Canada and the United States. It had informed United of its intention to invest in Continental.

Air Canada's and PWA's troubles raise the question of whether Canada can sustain two major airlines. Max Ward, who learned that the country cannot sustain three, believes "there is insufficient business for two." Thus as a member of PWA's board, he supported a merger of PWA with Air Canada. "Even though Air Canada and Canadian have downsized capacity, there is still too much considering the size of the market. At the same time they have priced their fares too high," he says. "The combination has resulted in a lot of competitive capacity being flown below cost. It's nice to have competition, but economics do count, and both airlines are in serious financial trouble."

Hollis Harris insisted that "a country with a population the size of Canada's can no longer support two airlines. Among the industrialized nations, experience has shown that a country needs a population of more than one hundred million to achieve the economies of scale necessary to support more than one international flag carrier." Harris liked to point out that outside of Canada, only Japan and the United States with populations six to ten times larger had a multi-flag carrier policy. In making this comparison, he omitted mentioning that Japan used to have a monopolistic industry. But Japan Airlines, previously the sole international airline, now also flies domestically and All Nippon Airways, formerly the only domestic carrier, now flies internationally, too.

Even more importantly, Harris's argument is negated by recent changes in the airline industry structure of Australia, the country most similar to Canada in that both are large countries with relatively small populations who travel a great deal at home and abroad, primarily by plane. These changes refute his argument that a nation Canada's size can only sustain one major airline. Australia's international and domestic traffic ranks fifth in the world, and Canada's seventh.

As in Canada, Australia's airline industry has been deregulated. But, unlike in Canada, the Australian government has taken a greater role in ensuring airline competition. In September 1993, it gave privately-owned Ansett Airlines, formerly a domestic airline only, the right to compete internationally against Qantas, previously the sole international carrier. The policy change was set in motion with the September 1992 purchase by then state-owned Qantas of similarly state-owned Australian Airlines, a domestic airline that was Ansett's rival. Subsequently, Australian Airlines took the Qantas name. The combined airline's revenue is around $3.6 billion, equivalent to that of Air Canada.

Next, the government began to privatize Qantas with the sale of 25 percent in March 1993 to British Airways. That investment is akin to AMR's proposed investment in Canadian Airlines International. The rest of Qantas will be sold to the public in what will be the biggest share issue in Australia's history.

Ansett could become a formidable competitor to Qantas seeing that it has a big domestic business and two powerful, monied owners – News Corporation, the media empire controlled by world-famous Rupert Murdoch, and PNT, a large Australian transportation company. Thus, the Australian government obviously believes Australia – a country similar in size, population and travel habits to Canada – can support two airlines.

Of the eight global megacarriers expected to survive to the year 2000, just one has a country monopoly. The eight are British Airways, Lufthansa and Air France in Europe; American, United and Delta in the United States; and Japan Airlines and All Nippon Airways in the Far East. State-owned Air France is the only monopoly, and it is in trouble. In the fall of 1993 it was all but shut down by a strike over its plans to eliminate thousands of jobs and cut the wages of remaining workers. In addition, the airline's financial loss for the year was U.S.$1 billion.

Notwithstanding British Airways' prominence, it is by no means Britain's only airline. It faces stiff competition from Britannia Airways and Virgin Airways. Britannia, the United Kingdom's leading charter airline, is owned by a Canadian firm, The Thomson Corporation which is both one of the world's largest travel companies and one of its biggest newspaper publishers. Its newspapers include *The Globe and Mail* of Toronto.

In that Canada is so big and Canadians travel by air so much, there should be enough business for two major airlines and for Canadian consumers to thereby enjoy the benefits of competition. But Air Canada and PWA cannot survive solely on their own and their actions in forming strategic alliances show that they are well aware of this fact. As in many other businesses, strategic alliances are becoming popular in the airline industry because they make it possible for companies to share costs as well as technical and marketing experience either with or without an equity stake.

There are many important marketing benefits. First, the combined power is far greater than an airline could have on its own. Second, such alliances enable an airline to divert business from a competitor. For example, the marketing agreement between Air Canada and Cathay Pacific feeds Cathay Pacific Canadian traffic that might otherwise fly to Hong Kong via Canadian Airlines International. In return, Air Canada receives ongoing Canadian traffic from incoming Cathay Pacific flights. In other cases, competitors can gain from joining forces on certain routes. CAIL and Lufthansa have a marketing agreement even though both fly to and from Frankfurt and Western Canada, and to and from Munich and Toronto. CAIL benefits because passengers headed for Canada who fly on Lufthansa to the two German cities are often then placed on CAIL flights. In reverse, CAIL connects ongoing overseas passengers with Lufthansa flights once they reach Germany.

All told, Air Canada has sixteen strategic alliances with airlines around the world, of which its investment in Continental is the only instance in which it has an equity stake. CAIL has six such alliances, including the one with AMR. Unlike Air Canada, CAIL has no equity stake in a foreign airline.

While the AMR-CAIL equity alliance was under discussion, the number of such cross-border arrangements worldwide neared two dozen with the finalization of several significant deals. For example, British Airways acquired a 25-percent interest in US Air as well as in Qantas in 1993.

Strategic alliances are important if Canada is to continue to have two major airlines. But there are other issues that have to be resolved, and these are discussed in the next chapter.

CHAPTER SEVEN

Learning from the Crisis

After months of stalemate, the long-running savage conflict between Air Canada and PWA briefly appeared tantalizingly close to a resolution in the last weeks of 1993. But while there was lots of drama, for the most part the events were a rehash of past moves and counter-moves, and the end result was no progress whatsoever.

The flurry of activity began two weeks after the Liberals were elected as the new federal government. On November 9, Transport Minister Douglas Young offered to appoint a "facilitator" in line with Jean Chrétien's suggestion in August 1993 for such intervention. On November 24, the Competition Tribunal ruled that PWA-Canadian could withdraw from its hosting contract with Gemini, and gave PWA and the other Gemini partners until December 8 to negotiate a settlement. Otherwise, the Tribunal would issue an order on December 14 to dissolve Gemini.

On November 25, Young made good his November 9 offer by appointing Stanley Hartt as the government's facilitator. Hartt was an apt choice because of his background in law, government and business, as well as his familiarity with the airline crisis. A labour lawyer, he had been federal deputy minister of finance (1985-88) and chief of staff to Prime Minister Mulroney (1989-90). After the collapse of Robert Campeau's real estate empire, Hartt was appointed chairman, president and chief executive officer of the surviving part, renamed Camdev Corporation.

He was well versed about the airline crisis because he had been assigned as the federal government's observer to PWA's board following the then-Conservative government's $50-million loan guarantee to PWA. Coincidentally, that guarantee was announced on November 24, 1992, exactly one year before the Competition Tribunal's release of CAIL from Gemini. Hartt's mediation skills were then made use of by PWA and Craig Dobbin, the majority owner of Air Atlantic, a CAIL regional affiliate, in a 1992-93 disagreement over routes and frequencies between Air Atlantic and CAIL. After spending "a few hours with them," Hartt helped resolve the dispute by suggesting Air Atlantic be allocated a few additional flights.

Since Air Canada and PWA were still locked in combat during the Hartt talks on December 8, the Tribunal gave an extension until December 20, and if an agreement was not reached by then, set December 24 for dissolving Gemini. On December 10, Gemini and PWA reached an out-of-court settlement of Gemini's claim for $1.5 billion in damages for alleged fiduciary irresponsibility and for unlawful interference in its economic interest. The amount of the settlement was undisclosed; however, analysts placed it at only $500,000.

But while this issue was resolved, CAIL's withdrawal from Gemini continued to be hotly contested in the mediation sessions. Unable to achieve a compromise, Hartt announced on December 15 that the talks had failed. Since the participants had signed confidentiality agreements, the causes for the failure were not divulged. But, taking into consideration that Air Canada told the Tribunal it wanted Gemini dissolved in the event CAIL withdrew, Gemini's survival does not appear to have been the cardinal reason despite Air Canada's having made such a point of publicly saying Gemini must be saved. Nor does money seem to have been an obstacle. The Tribunal had stated that if it wound up having to dissolve Gemini, PWA-CAIL would only have to pay the direct costs involved in the transfer of its hosting contract. CAIL's prediction that the amount would be $700,000 was not contradicted by the other Gemini partners.

If Gemini's future and money were not the principal factors, by a process of elimination the root cause of the talks' collapse was likely Air Canada's effort to use PWA's predicament as a bargaining chip to once again attempt to gain access to CAIL's international routes. But PWA was equally determined not to be dismembered.

Following Hartt's announcement on December 15, both airlines instantly made it clear that their positions remained unchanged. Air Canada said it would appeal the Tribunal's November 24 ruling to the Federal Court of Appeal, and PWA said AMR had agreed to extend its December 31 deadline for its deal with CAIL to June 30, 1994.

Just one day after the talks ended, credence was given to the theory that Air Canada's primary target was to obtain PWA's overseas business when it somewhat sweetened its August 18 offer for CAIL's international routes. However, while the new offer promised $250 million cash, an improvement of $50 million from August, the rest of the terms were largely identical. Once again, the bulk of the transaction was to be in the form of the assumption of $800 million in debt or lease obligations for jets CAIL uses on its overseas routes. The timing of Air Canada's offer – just hours after it rejected another PWA attempt to buy its way out of Gemini – further substantiates the theory that obtaining PWA's overseas routes was its foremost objective. On December 21, PWA rejected the offer.

Thus, expectations were dashed that the Christmas Holiday spirit of goodwill would result in a settlement of Canada's airline crisis. Instead, Air Canada and PWA were scheduled to clash again in court over Gemini, this time on February 16 and 17, 1994 before the Federal Court of Appeal over appeals by Air Canada and Gemini against the Competition Tribunal's November 24 ruling. Air Canada's purpose continued to be, as Hollis Harris said, "to prevent Canadian from accomplishing its goal" of an alliance with AMR. The airline sent a pamphlet to its frequent fliers entitled "A Made in Canada" solution, advocating its various proposals to PWA. Just before Christmas, it also sent some analysts a booklet called "PWA/Canadian as a partner in Gemini – a tale of deceit," which, astonishingly, contained copies of memos written by PWA's Rhys Eyton.

In addition, Hollis Harris insisted that he was confident Air Canada would win at the February 16 and 17 hearing because "our lawyers believe we have solid legal grounds." So, it appeared to come as a complete surprise on January 26 when Air Canada announced it was dropping its appeal, clearing the way for the CAIL–AMR deal to proceed. CAIL employees said they were "thrilled" and "ecstatic." But their jubilation proved to be very shortlived for the next day Transport Minister Douglas Young declared that Air Canada would be designated by the government as a second carrier to Japan, flying to the new airport in Osaka, scheduled to open in September 1994. Following his statement, Air Canada said that it also "expects" second-carrier designation to Hong Kong along with the rights to develop routes to China. (CAIL flies to Hong Kong, Tokyo, Nagoya which is some distance from Osaka, Shanghai and Beijing). Thus, the battle between Air Canada and PWA moved into a new arena – Asia, the fastest-growing market worldwide in air travel.

On February 15, one day before they were to appear before the Federal Court, Gemini and Covia dropped their appeals and Air Canada said it would create a new company – Galileo Canada – that will employ many Gemini workers. As did Gemini, it will pay to use the Apollo software of Galileo International, in which Air Canada and United Airlines, Covia's majority owner, are shareholders.

While Air Canada's January 26 announcement seemed unexpected in view of its continuing belligerency in the preceding weeks, there were several portents – albeit not from it – that it would change its strategy. On January 17, Gemini announced that its president, Paul Nelson, would resign January 31. On January 24, two days before Air Canada's about-face, CAIL's president, Kevin Jenkins, expressed concern about the possibility of Air Canada's getting a route to Japan. "We've been the ones to pioneer that route and we don't want it taken away just because of a fancy lobby," he said.

In that the government allocated Air Canada the Osaka route just one day after Air Canada dropped its litigation, Douglas Young was naturally asked if a deal had been struck between the airline and the government. "Let's not be naïve; everything is interconnected," he said, although denying any direct relation. To those who are not naïve, the two events, at the very least, seemed a remarkable coincidence. In return, CAIL will probably press for more routes into the United States; access is almost entirely dominated now by Air Canada. CAIL does not fly to any major eastern or midwestern U.S . cities. However, because the Canada-U.S. negotiations over air routes are in limbo, CAIL's hopes will not be realized in the near future.

Air Canada's withdrawal of its appeal may not only have been due to its apparent deal with the government. It also was a recognition that it would very likely lose both at the Federal Court level and at the Supreme Court, should it proceed further. On July 30, 1993, the Federal Court of Appeal said the Competition Tribunal had the authority to release PWA from Gemini, and on October 14, the Supreme Court refused to hear Air Canada's request that it reconsider the lower court's decision.

In the short term, PWA, Air Canada, the government, Gemini and consumers are winners. PWA–CAIL survives and CAIL's deal with AMR will likely be closed in April, two months early. Although Gemini will cease to exist November 5, it will be recreated. Air Canada achieves entry to Asia which it has coveted for years. The government, avoiding the political nightmare of a PWA collapse and the resultant unemployment of nearly fifteen thousand people, can portray itself as a saviour of competition in Canada's airline industry. Consumers win because there will still be two competitive airlines.

But in the long term, the outlook is for more troubled skies. CAIL faces potential erosion of its Asian routes, its most lucrative market. It now carries about 60 percent of the 300,000 passengers who travel between Canada and Japan. CAIL has never disclosed how much money it makes from its routes to Japan, Hong Kong and China. Airline analysts refuse to speculate. But one indicator of the routes' importance is that in 1991 CAIL began flying two large jumbo jets, seating 392 people, to Tokyo and Hong Kong and in 1992, it introduced a third. These jets – the Boeing 747–400 – are the world's largest commercial aircraft.

Although Air Canada's first choice in Japan was Tokyo's Narita Airport, there are currently no available landing slots there and many other airlines want access, too. Still, Air Canada undoubtedly will continue to press for

Tokyo as well as Osaka. In turn, CAIL is shut out of Osaka now that Air Canada has that market. Consequently, CAIL will continue to have to fly to Nagoya and provide free bus service to Osaka, a four-hour trip.

Considering that air travel between Canada and Japan has declined from 400,000 in 1989 to 300,000 currently, it is unlikely that there will be enough business for Air Canada plus CAIL plus Japan Airlines which also flies the route, and probably All Nippon Airways. All Nippon, JAL's rival, will likely gain access in exchange for Air Canada's becoming a second Canadian carrier to Japan. The result will be overcapacity and probably price wars, the same problems that have slashed the profitability of Air Canada and CAIL due to their fierce domestic competition.

Moreover, the industry is beset by other dilemmas. In order to reduce continued overcapacity at home, the airlines may cut back their number of flights, so that while still frequent, they will no longer be back-to-back. This would result in either a further decrease in employment or demands for more wage concessions or both. It would also lessen the choice in flights for consumers. In addition, PWA shareholders face dilution of the value of their shares as a result of PWA's debt-restructuring plan, although they will be issued a compensatory number of shares. Since both airlines are still in deep trouble financially, they probably will increase fares somewhat as part of their efforts to restore profitability. Should all these developments occur, the government of the day will be under pressure from the airlines and the public to intervene.

* * *

Even with their current dispute resolved, Air Canada and PWA are far from fully recovered financially. How well they do is of utmost importance to every Canadian since air travel by Canadians ranks seventh in the world, although Canada's population ranks only thirty-first in size. Both airlines have much to do to improve cost efficiency. Moreover, there are two important questions awaiting resolution that will affect Canadian consumers as well as the airlines: What is the outlook for greater competition and should the industry be reregulated?

The airlines' cutbacks in capacity and employment have received much attention; however, there are numerous other cost-saving measures they have also undertaken. They have transferred lower volume routes to their regional affiliates which fly smaller planes, cancelled unprofitable international flights, centralized purchasing and training by their regionals, reduced their number of reservation offices, improved handling of baggage and cargo, and sped up maintenance-cycle time. Nevertheless, there are still more areas in which the airlines could cut costs.

Some of these will remain intact because their elimination would result in the loss of customers. For example, although frequent-flier free-mileage programs sharply diminish revenue, they are a powerful tool in building consumer loyalty. Therefore, they will remain untouched. But, there are other areas in which the airlines can do peripheral trimming to shrink costs without annoying travellers, such as the outlay on meals. Meal costs could be substantially reduced if the airlines were to decrease the number of alternatives from the dozens now available. Many are virtually indistinguishable as, for instance, variations of vegetarian and low fat/low calorie/low salt and gluten-free menus.

On flights over ninety minutes, business and first-class travellers have a choice of two entrées, and over three hours, a choice of three. People who pay business and first-class fares do so partly to be better wined and dined than those flying in economy. For those who enjoy the frills, it is the only way to fly.

On the other hand, airlines that do not offer all this pampering tend to be more profitable. For example, Southwest, the most profitable U.S. airline, has done well by deliberately limiting what it does. "It confines itself to the southwest states and is a no-frills, low-fare, lost-cost carrier," explains Raymond Neidl, associate director and airline industry analyst at Furman Selz, a New York investment dealer. "It does not reserve seats, serve meals or accept interline traffic, but it does provide simple, point-to-point service on a young fleet of planes at a low, simplified price. It has succeeded by targeting sales to make a profit and not to simply capture market share."

All Southwest flights are under three hours. Its philosophy is that customers can eat before or after their trip in contrast to Air Canada and CAIL flights which provide meals on flights over ninety minutes – half the length of the longest Southwest flight. However, Southwest does serve a limited selection of beverages and a tiny package of peanuts, a staple on many airline flights to the irritation of most passengers who regard the peanuts as tantamount to nothing.

In general, Canada's airlines tend to spend more on passenger food service than U.S. carriers, according to Statistics Canada. In 1990, the year Statistics Canada chose for its comparison, CAIL spent an average of $14 per passenger and Air Canada, $13.86, whereas the American average was less than $6. Moreover, Statistics Canada found that on flights of equivalent distances, Air Canada and CAIL are more likely than American carriers to serve meals. Statistics Canada did a further comparison based on the January 1, 1992 Official Airline Guide. On the 72 daily flights from Ottawa to Toronto, a distance of 364 kilometres, breakfast was served on sixteen, lunch on four, and a snack on fourteen. By contrast, there were 180 daily

Washington-New York City flights, a distance of 342 to 367 kilometres depending upon the airports of departure and arrival. None served breakfast or lunch; fifty-four served a snack.

Overall, CAIL and Air Canada outspend most of their American counterparts on total passenger service. In turn, they are surpassed by Singapore Airlines and British Airways, according to Statistics Canada. Both of these airlines are consistently ranked among the world's best airlines in the annual business poll conducted by *Euromoney*, a British business magazine read internationally. However, the results have to be treated with some skepticism since some airlines appear on both the best and worst lists. For example, in 1992, British Airways placed first on both! Air Canada and CAIL were not on either list.

There has to be a happy medium between small packages of peanuts and huge meals fit for royalty so that customers do not starve but airlines still make money. Some airlines are penny-pinching in almost imperceptible ways. For example, American Airlines is serving lighter meals, and Northwest Airlines saved $67,000 by grinding its coffee more finely and $240,000 by only providing spoons with cereal.

The airlines do charge economy passengers for drinks on some flights, but the fee is more of an effort to prevent over-drinking than to generate revenue. Also, since the flight attendants put the money in their pockets rather than in a cash register and are on the honour system to turn in the money at the end of the day, there is no way of tracking the real total.

While the way to customers' hearts may indeed be through their stomachs, all-round good service is more important to the majority. However, what passengers consider paramount on short flights differs from their priorities on longer ones. By realizing the distinction, the airlines can improve their cost efficiency as well as satisfy travellers. For example, people making short-distance flights for brief stays usually have carry-on luggage at the most and tend to arrive at the airport shortly before their flight. Consequently, what they want are a quick check-in with no lineup and a quick walk to the departure gate.

By contrast, people flying overseas usually have at least one suitcase and security clearance regulations require them to check in well in advance of their flight. Thus, they want an express check-in and then a comfortable departure lounge.

Besides realizing that the needs of short- and far-distance and brief- and long-stay travellers should be handled differently, airlines must determine the nature of their target audience and market themselves accordingly. For instance, Southwest Airlines has remained profitable in these harsh economic times by concentrating on bargain-hunters willing to do without meals in exchange for low fares. But carriers like Air Canada and CAIL which fly regionally, nationally and internationally have a stiffer profitability challenge. One way they can tackle it is to schedule their flights to coincide with the peak travel times of their higher-paying customers –businesspeople who pay full economy, business or first-class fares. Any empty seats could then be sold to leisure travellers paying discount fares.

By contrast, on off-days and hours, more discount fares would be sold. "Leisure travellers are important, but they should be regarded as a by-product, just as sausages are a by-product of steak and chops," says analyst Tony Hine of ScotiaMcLeod.

*   *   *

If CAIL had failed, both of Canada's two major charter airlines – Air Transat and Canada 3000 – would have considered replacing it as a competitor to Air Canada, but only on some cross-country routes. An aviation consultant, testifying on behalf of Air Canada during the National Transportation Agency's 1993 hearings regarding AMR's investment in CAIL, contended that the climate was favourable for the establishment of small airlines. According to him, these new airlines could link up with the charters as a competitive option to Air Canada. However, it should be noted that the objective of Air Canada's witnesses was to prove that if CAIL should fail, Air Canada would not have a monopoly.

The consultant who made the prediction about a coalition of the charters and small, local airlines was Harold Shenton, a former airline executive at CP Air, Pan American Airlines, and Trans World Airlines; he is now a vice-president at Avmark, a foremost U.S. aviation consulting firm. Shenton described Canada's air travel patterns as being conducive to the creation of small airlines serving a "niche" market. "Depending on locale, between 70 and 90 percent of Canada's air traffic is regional, compared to only 50 percent in the United States," he said. "The top twenty-five Canadian city pairs (traffic between two cities) account for about 56 percent of all scheduled domestic passenger traffic, in sharp contrast to the United States where the proportion is only 14 percent." He concluded that, consequently, there would be enough point-to-point traffic for small airlines.

Shenton further suggested that the conditions were good to enter the business because the oversupply of planes had caused a steep decline in their value. "The best time to start an airline is not when the market is booming but when it is depressed because of the ready supply of cheap aircraft, the availability of skilled labour displaced from failing or shrinking airlines, and empty gates at some airports," he said. The scenario he portrayed can be compared to real estate investors buying prime properties at bargain prices during tough times in the expectation that their value will skyrocket when the economy improves.

However, neither Air Transat nor Canada 3000 could have provided Canadians with comprehensive competition to Air Canada due to several insurmountable obstacles they faced. First, both are only a fraction of the size of Air Canada. Air Transat, the larger of the two, just has twelve planes; Air Canada has 115. Second, these charter airlines have lower overhead because they use planes fifteen or more years old and crowd in as many people as possible. Charter customers tolerate the discomfort since fares are low. But on a regular basis, travellers want newer, more comfortable planes.

Therefore, to compete against Air Canada, Air Transat and Canada 3000 would have had to spend heavily on fleet expansion and modernization. Even so, they would have been at a disadvantage, considering that they would have lacked competitive frequent-flier programs and well-located airport space – problems that Wardair was unable to overcome when it attempted to transform itself from a charter to a scheduled operation.

Air Transat and Canada 3000 are unlikely to engage in head-on competition against both Air Canada and CAIL, especially as there are two recent examples of charter airlines that died in their attempt to do so – Wardair and Nationair. Moreover, with the notable exception of Wardair, charter airlines have not lasted long in Canada. Eight charter operations, including Nationair, have failed since 1990. Moreover, although Nationair had become Canada's largest airline charter operator and third-largest carrier, it was dwarfed in size by CAIL and Air Canada. It had only fifteen planes; Air Canada had more than seven times that number.

Some proponents of competition maintain it could be injected into Canada's airline industry through granting foreign airlines "cabotage" rights, enabling them to fly not only to and from Canada but also between Canadian cities. Cabotage is a key component of the proposed "open skies" agreement between Canada and the United States which is nowhere near being signed, even though it was suggested back in 1990.

Opponents to cabotage argue that it would have several negative ramifications. First, the increased choice would be confined to a limited number of places, notably larger cities where there is enough potential business. Thus, the majority of Canadians would not benefit. Second, the additional flights could aggravate the industry's overcapacity problem. Third, there is no guarantee that other countries would provide Canadian carriers reciprocal cabotage rights. Consequently, the Canadian airlines would be vulnerable to loss of revenue at home with no certainty of compensatory business in the rest of the world. Fourth, and perhaps most importantly, foreign carriers have expressed no interest whatsoever in obtaining Canadian cabotage rights.

There are many who believe the government should restore regulation to the airline industry. The foremost advocates are the airline unions, both for the sake of thousands of workers who have lost their jobs in recent years and for their own sake because their memberships and union dues have been decimated as a result.

For example, the Canadian Air Line Pilots Association's membership has declined by 15 percent due to layoffs of pilots employed for ten years or longer at Air Canada and CAIL. CALPA's anger was expressed in its submission to the National Transportation Act Review Commission's 1993 study of the first five years of deregulation in Canada. The submission read: "Deregulation reduces competition because the weakest are eliminated. We now have two heavyweights fighting it out to the point where both are bleeding and exhausted. But in the name of continued competition, the Commission's only advice to the contestants is: 'Keep going; more of what ails you will be good for you.'"

The Canadian Union of Public Employees, which represents flight attendants, and the Canadian Auto Workers, which represents reservation agents, called deregulation "a disaster" in a joint-position paper issued in the summer of 1993. "For workers, deregulation has meant layoffs, job insecurity, poorer working conditions, wage freezes and cuts, and a climate of fear in the workplace," the paper said.

In addition to the unions, the Council of Canadians and some politicians and industry analysts maintain reregulation is necessary. The Council of Canadians berates deregulation for "bringing chaos and crisis to the Canadian airline industry." However, the airlines have not pressed for reregulation.

While a broad spectrum of people favour reregulation, there is no consensus as to what form it should take. The unions tend to support a complete return to the past of government controls over fares, routes and capacity. But industry analysts who believe reregulation is necessary think it should be linked to the issue of capacity and be enforced only on a temporary basis until the overcapacity problem is eliminated.

During the recent federal election, the New Democratic Party said that, if elected, it would reintroduce government controls through a graduated system of regulation of fares and capacity. The NDP would have allowed carriers to begin competitive service on routes on which rivals' planes were more than 80 percent full; below that level, carriers would have had to obtain government permission to enter a market.

The Reform Party opposed any government financial help to the industry. The Liberals said "a certain level of regulation" was necessary to prevent "predatory pricing, predatory scheduling, and other anti-competitive behaviour."

The Liberals' vagueness was matched by that of the Conservatives. Transport Minister Jean Corbeil made only one speech in Parliament regarding the airline crisis and that was back on November 24, 1992. Moreover, it was principally a review of the already well-known problems. He did, however, make a brief reference to whether there should be a "reinforcement of our regulatory framework." His conclusion was merely that it "may be necessary to suggest a recalibration of the framework to ensure that it will promote a healthy competitive environment for the airline industry."

Not once in the eleven months that followed, right up to the October 25, 1993 election, did Corbeil define what he meant by "recalibration." Staffers in his office and at the National Transportation Agency expressed bafflement when asked to explain what he meant. Efforts by the Opposition to obtain some clarification during Question Periods in Parliament failed on repeated occasions. All that Corbeil would reply was that it was up to the industry to solve its problems.

Although deregulation has contributed to the airlines' difficulties, it is unlikely that reregulation will occur due to the influence of global factors. Just as deregulation came to Canada primarily because it existed next door in the United States, it will likely continue now that deregulation is spreading around the world. "Regulation is gone; the current liberalization is spreading worldwide," Pierre Jeanniot, director general of the International Air Transport Association (IATA), emphatically states. "It is impossible to return to a gone day."

But while the clock cannot be turned back, much can be learned from the industry's crisis that could help prevent a recurrence. The industry's chief characteristic has always been its fight to survive. The airlines have fought to survive at one another's expense. Privately-owned ones have battled against publicly-owned ones. Workers have striven to save their jobs. Executives have manoeuvred to survive in power struggles. In addition, the survival of competition and thereby a choice for consumers has been at stake.

Throughout the years, Canada's airline industry has bounced between losses and profitability. But what stands out is that the worst losses – those since 1990 – have occurred under what former PWA president Donald Watson derisively describes as "business suit people." As he says, they have been "no more successful and less visionary" than predecessors such as Grant McConachie and Russell Baker who lacked a university education but had abundant entrepreneurial drive. His conclusion could readily be applied to other businesses as well.

Today's executives at Air Canada and PWA are well-educated, well-trained and well-intentioned, but they made misjudgments that resulted in overcapacity, overemployment and overexpansion. However, they were by no means alone in misreading the market; the same mistakes were made by their counterparts around the world.

Canada's airline crisis is an ugly example of how one company can seek to survive at the expense of another. Air Canada wanted to return to the past when it was the dominant airline by taking over all or part of PWA. PWA wanted to survive through the dissolution of Gemini even though Gemini was solvent. Workers at each airline cast aside union solidarity regarding nationwide protection of airline jobs because very understandably, they considered their personal survival as more important to themselves and their families. Nine thousand workers have been laid off by Air Canada and PWA since 1989.

In addition, the crisis demonstrated the harmful repercussions of government waffling. Although the early appointment of a mediator could have produced a solution, the Conservative government under both Brian Mulroney and Kim Campbell allowed the crisis to drag on.

Hopefully, the crisis has made it clear that an end must be put to the frequent turnover in ministers of transport, so as to provide some measure of experience. During the nine years the Conservatives were in power, there were five ministers of transport. The longest the position was held was a mere two years.

While it could be argued that the replacement rate was unimportant since government policy remained the same, the multiple changes did have a significant impact considering that it takes a while for anybody to become knowledgeable about a field. Only a few of the ministers were well informed about transportation issues before their appointment.

Jean Corbeil, the minister from 1991 until the Liberals defeated the Conservatives in the October 25, 1993 election, was an insurance broker before being elected to Parliament. He was briefly minister of labour from June 1989 until February 1990 when he became minister of state for transport en route to his April 1991 appointment as minister of transport.

There are two people in Jean Chrétien's Cabinet with transportation expertise – John Manley, who had been the Liberals' transport critic before they won the recent election, and Lloyd Axworthy, who had been minister of transport in 1983-84. Nevertheless, Manley was made minister of industry, and Axworthy, minister, human resources. As minister of transport, Chrétien appointed Douglas Young, a lawyer, who served in the New Brunswick Legislature from 1978 and became minister of fisheries and aquaculture in 1987 prior to being elected to the House of Commons in 1988. It is common procedure for prime ministers not to appoint people with in-depth knowledge of a field to a portfolio; instead, ministerial appointments often are based on political factors such as cross-country geographical representation. Young is the only Cabinet member from New Brunswick and one of the three ministers from Atlantic Canada in the twenty-three member Cabinet. Moreover, after only a month in the job, he did what Corbeil had not done in more than a year: he intervened, through the appointment of mediator Stanley Hartt, to try to resolve the crisis.

*   *   *

The continued existence of the two major airlines is of vital importance to Canadians because it provides them with a competitive choice. Competition means better service and keeps fares from rising even higher. Unfortunately, as the airlines reduce over-capacity, fares may go up somewhat in a profit improvement measure. Another benefit of competition is that if one airline should be shut down by a strike, Canadians would not be stranded because the other would still be flying. In that Australia, a country of comparable size, population, and travel habits to Canada, has two competitive airlines, Canada should also be able to sustain two.

A further lesson that can be derived from the crisis is that airline executives cannot be insular in their thinking. From their earliest days, Canada's airlines have profited from the experience of others. For example, C.D. Howe, "Mr. TCA," was American-born and that airline's first executives were mainly American. Today, airlines around the world, like many other businesses, are acknowledging that to stay alive they must form transnational strategic alliances. AMR's investment in CAIL and Air Canada's in Continental are part of this trend. Using again what is going on in Australia as a benchmark, it should be borne in mind that Qantas, the well-known Australian airline, is now partly owned by British Airways.

Although the airline industry has been in deep trouble worldwide and not just in Canada, plane travel has become so much a part of our lives that it is here to stay. "Airline travel is indispensable to the world due to the growth of business globalization and tourism," IATA's Pierre Jeanniot says.

For the sake of its employees, shareholders, lenders and the Canadian travelling public, it is to be hoped that Canada's airline industry has learned from the crisis of the last few painful years. But, unfortunately, the indications are otherwise. For more than fifty years, Air Canada has battled its rivals, and while the fight over the CAIL–AMR deal and Gemini is over, it has given birth to fresh hostilities that all too likely will soon plunge the industry into crisis again.

Appendix I

KEY DATES

1919   Parliament extends Canadian Pacific Railway's (CPR) charter to allow it to enter the airline business.

1920   Newly formed Canadian Air Force makes first transcontinental flight across Canada.

1926   James Richardson establishes Western Canada Airways.

1927   Canadian Pacific Railway becomes one of six shareholders in Aviation Corporation of Canada, a consolidation of four small aircraft operators.

1930   Western Canada Airways and Aviation Corporation merge under the name Canadian Airways in which Richardson, Canadian Pacific and Canadian National Railways are the shareholders.

1936   Federal Department of Transport established.

1937   Trans-Canada Air Lines (TCA) established by federal government as wholly owned subsidiary of Canadian National Railways.

1940-41 Canadian Pacific buys Canadian Airways and nine small airline companies.

1942   Canadian Pacific consolidates the ten companies as Canadian Pacific Airlines (CPAL).

1943   TCA begins transatlantic service of mail, important cargo, and official passengers.

1945   – TCA begins commercial transatlantic service.

           – Establishment of Central British Columbia Airways (CBCA), a forerunner of Pacific Western Airlines.

1948   CPAL obtains its first international route – to Sydney, Australia – when TCA turns down the route.

1949   – CPAL begins flights to Tokyo and Hong Kong.

           – CPAL moves its headquarters from Montreal to Vancouver.

1953   – CBCA renamed Pacific Western Airlines (PWA).

           – Wardair established as charter airline.

1958   Federal Air Transport Board rules that CPAL can make one transcontinental flight a day.

1959   CPAL begins transcontinental flights.

1960   TCA suggests a TCA-CPAL merger.

1964   – Federal government recommends an integrated TCA-CPAL international system.

          – TCA renamed Air Canada.

1966-69   Government divides Canada into five regional markets served by different carriers – PWA, Transair, Nordair, Quebecair, Eastern Provincial Airways. They are restricted regarding types of aircraft and routes. Wardair's charter routes not to interfere with CPAL's and Air Canada's.

1967   Government allows CPAL to double its transcontinental capacity and, then, to continue to grow to 25 percent of the total.

1968   CPAL renamed CP Air.

1973   Air Canada considers buying Wardair.

1974   Alberta government acquires PWA.

1976   Alberta government moves PWA's headquarters from Vancouver to Calgary.

1978   – Air Canada acquires majority interest in Nordair.

          – Deregulation begins in United States.

1979   Federal government ends restrictions on CP Air's transcontinental market share.

1983   Alberta government privatizes PWA.

1984   – Air Canada sells Nordair to Innocan (a Montreal venture capital firm whose investors include Air Canada's and Canadian National's pension funds) and a Nordair employee group.

          – CP Air buys Eastern Provincial Airways.

1985   CP Air buys majority interest in Nordair. Quebec government retains the remainder.

1986   – August: Quebecair bought by Nordair Metro, a Quebec commuter airline 35 percent-owned by Nordair.

          – December: PWA announces it will buy CP Air.

1987   – February: PWA acquires CP Air for $300 million.

– April: PWA and CP Air operations combined under the name Canadian Airlines International.

– July: Air Canada and PWA jointly form the Gemini computer reservation system.

1988   – New federal National Transportation Act deregulates government route and price controls.

– Government begins to privatize Air Canada; 43 percent sold to the public.

– Federal Competition Tribunal investigates whether Gemini should be dissolved on grounds that it is allegedly anti-competitive.

1989   – PWA acquires Wardair for $250.8 million.

– CAIL eliminates 1,900 jobs, of which 1,017 are former Wardair employees.

– Remaining 57 percent of Air Canada privatized.

– Competition Tribunal approves AC-PWA Gemini arrangement.

– Covia, a computer reservation system 50 percent-owned by United Airlines and the rest by a number of American and European airlines, becomes a 33 percent partner in Gemini.

1990   – CAIL and Wardair are merged.

– Air Canada eliminates 2,900 jobs.

– "Open skies" talks announced between Canada and the United States; the goal is almost unlimited access for carriers to operate in both countries.

1991   – Starting in fall of 1991 and continuing into winter of 1992, Air Canada and PWA discuss (1) an outright merger or (2) Air Canada's purchasing PWA's international routes.

– Heavy losses reported by Air Canada ($318 million) and PWA ($162 million). Both airlines reduce jobs.

1992   – March 12: PWA and AMR, parent of American Airlines, sign a letter of intent under which AMR would acquire a one-third equity interest in CAIL and 25 percent voting interest (the maximum allowed under Canadian rules regarding foreign ownership of airlines). In return, CAIL would buy marketing and management services from AMR and transfer from Gemini to AMR's computerized reservation system, Sabre.

- March 19: PWA terminates merger talks with Air Canada. In response, Air Canada registers an objection with the National Transportation Agency that control of CAIL would effectively pass into U.S. hands.

- April 3: Gemini tells CAIL it will sue for breach of contract if CAIL transfers to AMR's Sabre system.

- May: Air Canada says it will eliminate 250 management positions and 100 administrative and technical support positions.

- June: PWA stops dividend payments on some preferred shares.

- July 1: Air Canada announces further job reductions, saying it will eliminate 9 percent of its workforce.

- July 3: Gemini files complaint with Competition Tribunal that Sabre is engaged in predatory pricing in Canada contrary to the federal Competition Act.

- July 27: -PWA terminates discussions with AMR and resumes merger discussions with Air Canada, on a non-exclusive basis. AMR says it is still interested in pursuing an alliance with CAIL.

  - Directors of wholly-owned subsidiaries of PWA resign, but remain on the board of PWA itself. Their resignations are prompted by concerns over potential personal liability exposure in the event of insolvency.

- August 10: Council of Canadian Airline Employees formed to provide PWA with a capital infusion through payroll deductions.

- August 17: PWA rejects a formal merger proposal from Air Canada and revives its attempt to link with AMR.

- August 19: Air Canada says it will begin a marketing alliance with United Airlines in October.

- August 27: Air Canada and Air Partners, a Texas investment group, offer to invest U.S.$400 million in Continental Airlines, a U.S. airline operating under U.S. bankruptcy protection since December 1990.

- August 31: PWA launches a court case in Alberta to have Gemini declared insolvent, thereby freeing CAIL to transfer to AMR's Sabre system.

- September 1: PWA's representative on Gemini's board proposes that Gemini be dissolved.
- September 2: Air Canada makes a new merger proposal to PWA. Under the merger, Air Canada's shareholders would have 60 percent of the new company and PWA's 40 percent. At least 6,000 jobs would be eliminated. Deadline of September 9 given for decision.
- September 8: Air Canada agrees to provide up to $100 million in "bridge" financing to PWA if a pre-merger agreement is reached.
- September 9: Council of Canadian Airlines Employees offers to invest up to $150 million in exchange for shares if PWA agrees to pursue AMR's proposal, which would mean fewer job losses. However, PWA instead accepts Air Canada's offer.
- September 10: Competition Tribunal begins an inquiry into proposed Air Canada-PWA merger.
- September 23: Air Canada forms a marketing alliance with Air France, effective April 1993.
- October 6: Air Canada and Air Partners increase their Continental Airlines offer from $400 million to $425 million. (Actual final price is $450 million.)
- October 8: Air Canada and PWA sign a pre-merger agreement.
- October 27: Air Canada and PWA announce their boards have not approved the operating, financing and transaction plan developed by their merger committees but that discussions between them are continuing.
- November 3: Air Canada terminates its October 8 pre-merger agreement with PWA, saying the agreement would not produce a "viable" merged airline.
- November 5: Federal Bureau of Competition Policy recommends that Competition Tribunal's 1989 consent order regarding Gemini be changed or rescinded so that the proposed CAIL-AMR deal, conditional on CAIL switching to AMR's Sabre, can proceed.
- November 9: Continental Airlines accepts Air Canada-Air Partners investment offer.
- November 10: Alberta Court "stays" proceedings in court case launched August 31 by PWA to have Gemini declared insolvent.

- November 12: Gemini files $1-billion lawsuit against PWA claiming breach of fiduciary duty and $500-million lawsuit against both PWA and AMR claiming unlawful interference in Gemini's economic interest.
- November 17: PWA files a $1.5-billion lawsuit against Air Canada, alleging predatory pricing practices in 1992 "in order to drive CAIL out of the marketplace."
- November 19: Royal Commission on National Passenger Transportation releases its report. It calls for less government involvement in subsidizing transportation.
- November 24:
- Federal government says it will provide $50 million in interim loans to PWA.
- PWA launches court proceedings in Ontario to have Gemini declared insolvent.
- CAIL cuts managers' pay by 20 percent.
- November 29: PWA suspends principal and interest payments to most creditors for five months but continues to meet day-to-day obligations to trade creditors.
- December 2: Covia, a 33 percent partner in Gemini, launches a $1.2-billion lawsuit against PWA, alleging PWA breached its fiduciary duties as a Gemini partner.
- December 18: Alberta government provides $50 million and British Columbia's $20 million in loan guarantees to help PWA in its restructuring.
- December 22: Air Canada obtains a $5-million contract to modify Continental planes at Air Canada's Winnipeg facilities.
- December 29: PWA and AMR sign a "strategic alliance," conditional on CAIL's transfer to AMR's Sabre system.

1993
- February 23: Air Canada proposes a two-year, 5 percent wage cut for all employees. Their wages already have been frozen for three years, The chairman says he will take a 10 percent cut.
- March 22:
  - National Transportation Agency begins hearings into proposed AMR investment in CAIL.
  - Nationair, Canada's largest airline charter operator, seeks bankruptcy.

- April 2: Ontario Court of Justice's General Division rejects PWA's lawsuit that Gemini be declared insolvent.
- April 22: Competition Tribunal rules it lacks authority to release PWA from Gemini. However, it supports PWA's position that Gemini can survive without Canadian but that Canadian "will likely fail" if it cannot complete its deal with AMR. The Tribunal says that if the federal Court of Appeal rules the Tribunal does have jurisdiction, it will then decide in favour of PWA. PWA says it will appeal.
- April 28: Air Canada becomes part owner of Continental Airlines.
- April 29:
  - Air Canada's chairman tells annual meeting he plans to reduce employment by 2,200 by the end of 1993.
  - PWA resumes payments to creditors.
- April 30: PWA reports a first-quarter loss of $107 million.
- May 7: Air Canada reports a first-quarter loss of $293 million.
- May 12: Nationair declared bankrupt.
- May 27: National Transportation Agency approves AMR investment in CAIL but deal still hinges on PWA's as yet unaccomplished withdrawal from Gemini.
- June 2: Air Canada appeals to the federal Cabinet to overrule the NTA's May 27 decision. Under the terms of the National Transportation Act, Cabinet has 30 days in which to decide – in this case, by June 27.
- June 23: Federal Cabinet decides not to overrule NTA's May 27 decision.
- June 26: Pilots' strike at Air Alliance, Air Canada's Quebec regional airline, grounds flights.
- July 29: PWA reports a second-quarter loss of $130.6 million.
- July 30: Federal Court of Appeal rules that Competition Tribunal does have authority to release PWA from Gemini. (See April 22.)
- August 5: Air Canada reports a $14-million profit for its second quarter, its first quarterly profit in almost two years.
- August 11: Ontario Court of Appeal upholds April 2, 1993 ruling of Ontario Court of Justice's General Division that rejected PWA's request that Gemini be declared insolvent.

- August 16:
  - Air Canada announces plans to buy 24 Canadair regional jets, valued between $400 and $500 million, with an option for 24 more. The jets seat 50 people, will be delivered in 1994, and will be used on flights between Canadian and U.S. cities.
  - Continental Airlines, of which Air Canada became part-owner in April 1993, reports U.S.$24.4 million loss in first quarter of that ownership. It says it will cut 2,500 jobs and discontinue service to nine cities, including Vancouver.
- August 18: Air Canada offers $1 billion for Canadian Airlines International's international routes. The $1 billion would consist of $200 million in cash and the assumption of $800-million worth of debt and lease obligations on eight CAIL planes. CAIL chairman Rhys Eyton calls the offer "a diabolical plot to kill" CAIL.
- August 24: PWA rejects Air Canada's August 18 offer.
- August 27: Close to 97 percent of PWA's shareholders vote in favour of company's survival restructuring plan.
- September 28: Competition Tribunal says it will reexamine the Gemini issue in November, following the October 25 federal election.
- October 7: Air Canada asks Federal Court of Appeal to over-rule Competition Tribunal's decision that it will not hear new evidence at the November hearing. The new evidence is Air Canada's offer to buy PWA's international routes as an alternative to bankruptcy should AMR's investment in CAIL not occur.
- October 14: Supreme Court of Canada makes two rulings regarding Gemini:
  1) It refuses Air Canada's request that it reconsider the Federal Court of Appeal's July 30 ruling that the Competition Tribunal can resolve whether PWA can leave Gemini.
  2) It refuses PWA's request that it overrule the Ontario Court of Appeal's August 11 decision rejecting PWA's attempt to have Gemini declared insolvent, thereby enabling PWA to transfer to AMR's Sabre system.
- October 25: Liberals win federal election, defeating the Conservatives who had been in power since 1984.

- November 9:
  - Federal Court of Appeal rejects Air Canada's request that its bid for CAIL's international routes be considered at November 15 Competition Tribunal hearing in Gemini dispute.
  - Douglas Young, new federal transport minister, says he would appoint a mediator – but only at the airlines' request.
- November 11: Air Canada reports a $43-million profit for the three months ended September 30; it also announces plans to issue a prospectus for a $200 to $250-million share issue on November 15, the date the Competition Tribunal resumes its hearings in the Gemini dispute.
- November 15: Competition Tribunal resumes hearing into CAIL's request to release it from Gemini. Hearing to last the week; decision expected two weeks later.
- November 18: American Airlines' flight attendants strike, causing the cancellation of some flights. American is owned by AMR which has agreed to invest $246 million in Canadian Airlines.
- November 22: American Airlines' flight attendants end their strike after President Clinton convinced them and American's management to agree to binding arbitration.
- November 24:
  - Competition Tribunal rules that CAIL should be released from Gemini's "hosting" contract of CAIL's reservation system, thereby removing the chief obstacle to CAIL's strategic alliance with AMR.
  - PWA says it is seeking an extension to the December 31, 1993 deadline for closure of the deal with AMR.
  - PWA also reports a profit of $38.5 million for the three months ended September 30, its best quarter since the 1987 formation of Canadian Airlines.
- November 25: Following up on his November 9 offer, Transport Minister Douglas Young appoints a federal mediator to resolve the dispute between Air Canada and PWA. He is Stanley Hartt, a business executive who was chief of staff (1989-90) to Prime Minister Mulroney.
- December 8: Competition Tribunal extends its December 8 deadline to December 20 for Air Canada and PWA to reach a negotiated settlement following its November 24 ruling.

Otherwise, the Tribunal will proceed to dissolve Gemini on December 24, effective November 1994.

– December 10: PWA and Gemini reach an out-of-court settlement in Gemini's $1-billion lawsuit of November 12, 1992, alleging breach of fiduciary duties. Settlement also reached in Gemini's $500-million lawsuit against PWA and AMR alleging unlawful interference with Gemini's economic interest.

– December 15:

  – Federal government's mediation between Air Canada and PWA fails.

  – Air Canada says it will appeal Competition Tribunal's November 24 Gemini ruling.

  – PWA-CAIL says AMR has extended its offer until June 30, 1994.

– December 16:

  – PWA makes a new offer to buy its way out of Gemini. Air Canada rejects it.

  – Air Canada makes a new offer for PWA's international routes.

  – Federal government says it will not provide further financial assistance to PWA.

– December 21: PWA rejects Air Canada's December 16 offer.

– December 23: Gemini appeals Competition Tribunal's November 24 ruling.

1994   – January 26:

  – Air Canada says it is dropping its appeal of the Competition Tribunal's November 24 ruling, enabling the CAIL–AMR deal to proceed.

  – Transport Minister Douglas Young subsequently says the government will make a decision "very soon" on Air Canada's application to be designated a second carrier to Japan.

– January 27: Government designates Air Canada as second carrier to Japan.

– February 15:

  – Gemini and Covia drop their appeals of Competition Tribunal's ruling.

  – Air Canada says it will create a new reservation system, using much of Gemini's system.

Appendix II

TABLES

Air Canada and PWA "Families"

PWA Corporation (Holding Company)

Financial Results

1992 Cost Per Available Seat Mile

Air Canada and PWA "Families"

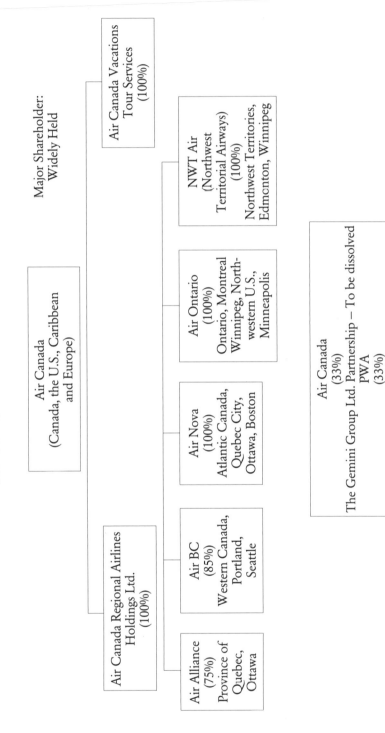

Major Shareholder: Widely Held

Air Canada
(Canada, the U.S., Caribbean and Europe)

Air Canada Vacations Tour Services
(100%)

Air Canada Regional Airlines Holdings Ltd.
(100%)

Air Alliance
(75%)
Province of Quebec, Ottawa

Air BC
(85%)
Western Canada, Portland, Seattle

Air Nova
(100%)
Atlantic Canada, Quebec City, Ottawa, Boston

Air Ontario
(100%)
Ontario, Montreal Winnipeg, North-western U.S., Minneapolis

NWT Air
(Northwest Territorial Airways)
(100%)
Northwest Territories, Edmonton, Winnipeg

Air Canada
(33%)
The Gemini Group Ltd. Partnership – To be dissolved
PWA
(33%)

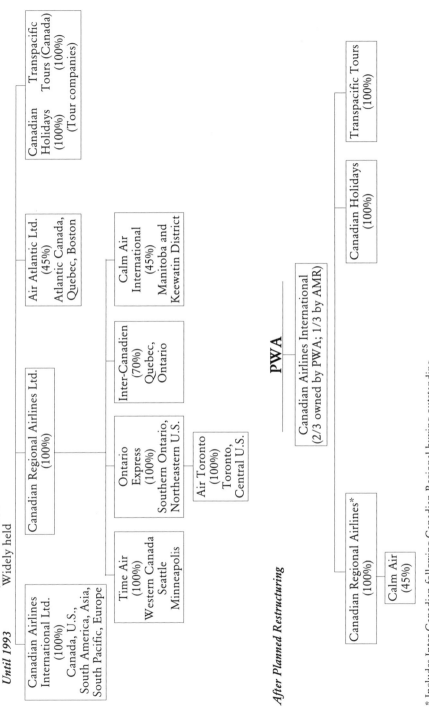

Financial Results (1)

	Air Canada					PWA				
	1992	1991	1990	1989	1988	1992	1991	1990	1989	1988
Operating revenues ($ millions)	3,501	3,485	3,899	3,618	3,404	2,877	2,871	2,746	2,649	2,284
Profit (loss) ($ millions)	(454)	(218)	(74)	149	89	(543)	(162)	(15)	(56)	30
Number of employees[1] (000)	18.2	20.6	23.1	23.2	22.6	14.6	15.6	16.0	16.5	13.1
Share Price ($) High	8.50	10.38	13.00	14.88	8.25	6.25	9.38	14.00	19.38	22.25
Low	2.20	6.63	7.25	7.25	7.00	0.54	4.00	6.75	13.38	13.63
Revenue Passenger Miles[2] (millions)	14,391	13,658	16,577	16,278	15,553	13,324	12,673	13,851	14,732	12,179
Available Seat Miles[3] (millions)	21,628	19,953	23,233	23,348	21,778	19,916	19,782	21,384	21,905	17,710
Yield per Revenue Passenger Mile[4]	16.3¢	17.4¢	16.8¢	16.3¢	15.7¢	16.2¢	16.9¢	16.0¢	14.6¢	14.4¢

[1] For PWA, the number given is for its Canadian Airlines International. PWA acquired Canadian Pacific Airlines in 1987 and Wardair in 1989.

[2] Revenue Passenger Miles: industry measure of traffic calculated by multiplying the number of revenue passengers by the number of miles they are carried.

[3] Available Seat Miles: industry measure of capacity calculated by multiplying the total number of seats available for revenue traffic by the miles flown.

[4] Yield: industry measure of performance; revenue per revenue passenger mile.

Financial Results (2)

Three Months to September 30

	Air Canada		PWA	
	1993	1992	1993	1992
Operating revenues	$1.03 billion	$1.0 billion	$883.6 million	$841.9 million
Profit (loss)	$43 million	($14 million)	$38.5 million	$2.7 million

Nine Months to September 30

	Air Canada		PWA	
	1993	1992	1993	1992
Operating revenues	$2.73 billion	$2.69 billion	$2.28 billion	$2.23 billion
Profit (loss)	($236 million)	($307 million)	($199.2 million)	($105.6 million)

Note: As the book went to press, both airlines announced their 1993 results. Air Canada had a loss of $326 million on revenues of $3.6 billion. PWA had a loss of $292 million on revenues of $2.97 billion.

1992 Cost Per Available Seat Mile

(The standard measure of cost competitiveness in the airline industry)

Canadian $/mile

	Wages	Fuel	Commission[1]	Depreciation and Amortization	Aircraft Rentals and User Fees	Other[2]	Total
Air Canada (consolidated)	$0.055	$0.022	$0.013	$0.010	$0.014	$0.056	$0.170
Air Canada (unconsolidated)	$0.049	$0.019	$0.010	$0.008	$0.011	$0.045	$0.142
PWA	$0.043	$0.018	$0.022	$0.006	$0.018	$0.043	$0.150
American Airlines	$0.040	$0.015	$0.010	$0.008	$0.012	$0.028	$0.113
United Airlines	$0.040	$0.015	$0.020	$0.006	$0.012	$0.025	$0.118
Delta Airlines	$0.043	$0.015	$0.011	$0.007	$0.009	$0.030	$0.115
US Air	$0.052	$0.015	$0.011	$0.006	$0.019	$0.038	$0.141

[1] Far East traffic accounts for a significant portion of PWA-Canadian Airlines International's and United's international business. In Asian markets, discounts to passengers are passed on by agents from their commissions with "bucket shops" giving deeper discounts.

[2] Other: Includes building rent and maintenance, advertising and promotion, terminal handling, crew meals and hotels, insurance costs, professional fees and services.

Source: ScotiaMcLeod

Index

Eichner, John, 89-90
Eyton, Rhys, 32-34, 45, 58-60, 73-74, 76-78, 82, 102-103, 106, 110, 113, 137
Eyton, Russ, 102

Fares, 6-7, 46-47, 54, 70, 78, 87, 90, 139-144, 147
Farley, James, 115
Fattedad, Sidney, 104-107
Federal Court of Appeal, 123, 136-137
Federal Industries, 28
First Marathon Securities, 112
Fischer, Duncan, 102
"Freedom To Move", 52, 54, 57-58, 64
Furman, Selz, 140

Galileo Canada, 137
Galileo International, 137
Garmaise, Steven, 112
Gemini Group Automated Distribution System, 40, 85, 104, 110-111, 119
    conflict over, 82, 86, 107, 115, 119, 122-124, 126-127, 135-136, 146; history of, 82, 120-122, 124-125, 130, 135-137, 146
General Electric Credit Corporation, 27, 83, 128
Getty, Don, 29
Gilbert, Walter, 15-16
Gilmore, Jack, 23-24, 33, 36, 41, 70
Gordon, Donald, 21
Gray, Ian, 10-13, 23-24, 34, 36, 38, 41-43, 44
Great Lakes Airlines. *See* Air Ontario

Hargrove, Basil (Buzz), 83, 106
Harris, Hollis, 6, 84, 93, 98, 109-111, 113, 127-131, 137
Harris, Iain, 62-64, 100

Harris, Rusty, 22
Hartt, Stanley, 135-136, 147
Hees, George, 18, 25, 50
Hine, Tony, 75, 88-89, 92-93, 111, 142
Hodgson, Stuart, 28
Horner, Hugh, 32
Howe, Clarence Decatur, 3-6, 11, 13-14, 34, 147

Industrial Development Bank, 17, 27
Innocan, 56
Inter-Canadien, 40, 102
International Air Transport Association, 89, 97, 145
International Civil Aviation Organization (ICAO), 69-70

Jamieson, John, 8
Japan Airlines, 131-132, 139
Jeanniot, Pierre, 50-51, 89, 93-95, 97, 145, 147
Jenkins, Kevin, 76-78, 126, 138

Kavafian, Jacques, 75, 111-113, 129
King, Egerton (Ed), 77
King, Mackenzie, 3-4, 8-9, 36, 40
KLM Royal Dutch Airlines, 43, 96
Korean Airlines, 96

Laidman, Dick, 22-23, 26-27
Lang, Otto, 31, 34-37, 52, 64-65
Larkin, Frederick (Ted), 74-75, 81, 87, 105, 116
Lethbridge Air Service, 45
Lévesque Beaubien Geoffrion, 75, 111
Limited Partnership Act, 121, 125
Little, Darcy, 61, 64, 100
Lougheed, Peter, 28-29, 32, 44
Love, R.B., 29-30
Lufthansa, 132

MacArthur, Douglas, 15
Manley, John, 146